Death & Back

Rob Aspinall

Copyright © 2017 by Rob Aspinall
All rights reserved.

No part of this book may be reproduced in any form or by any electronic or mechanical means, including information storage and retrieval systems, without written permission from the author, except for the use of brief quotations in a book review.

Prologue

I know what I said. I wasn't gonna do this anymore. I wasn't gonna do things like crack this guy in the face with a baseball bat. Or leave this moron bleeding in a pile of piss-stained rubbish.

I wasn't gonna do stuff like that.

I promised my daughter, Cassie, I'd jack in the criminal life. Go straight. No more fighting in the gutter.

But if I hadn't made the bloody promise, I wouldn't be here at all.

They say violence doesn't solve anything. And Cass would agree. But if you ask me, I reckon that's a big bag of bollocks. Violence solves a lot of things. It sorts out arguments. Divides up territory. Decides the pecking order. I mean, look at animals. They're always banging heads over this or that. Not as if they're holding hands and dancing around in Fluffy Rainbow Cloud Land. They've gotta scrap to survive.

So yeah, I said I wouldn't do this anymore. But I've got a damn good reason for giving these two losers a beating.

I'll elaborate more in a bit.

First, I've got a man to put in hospital.

Chapter 1

The sky was dark. The wind relentless. The black dinghy shook under the assault of every wave. Water slapped in over the sides. Ice cold, invading the inflated rubber floor.

Amira huddled with her elbows tucked to her ribs. Her hands on her knees. Her shins wedged against the large African man in front. The toes of someone's trainers digging into the small of her back.

All around her, she saw trembling bodies in cheap orange lifejackets.

The whites of eyes wide with fear and minds wired in spite of exhaustion. Amira willed the minutes, the seconds, the waves away. She breathed heavy through an open mouth. Attempted to quell the gathering squall inside her stomach.

It was no use. The rise and fall over each wave was unbearable. And they seemed to come at the dinghy from all sides.

Someone had already vomited. The smell unbearable.

The only reason Amira could think she hadn't been sick, was down to her stomach being empty of food. Two days without a bite to eat. And very little to drink.

On-board the dinghy, not an inch of rubber went spare. Which meant Amira couldn't see anything of the sea, or the land. Only the soulless sky.

She wondered if the unseen person steering the dinghy was off course. Or even worse—lost.

Amira would have asked him had she been able to move or make herself heard over the cross-chatter of languages. She didn't understand much. But she heard a few words in Arabic from two men sat on the far right edge of the dinghy. One man terrified of falling over the side—he couldn't swim. His friend reassuring him—the sea was warm, they had lifejackets, it *couldn't* be much longer.

The friend sounded as if he was trying to convince himself.

So she hung on, her mouth drier than the Hamad desert. Her mind in a sleep-deprived fog.

Until a glimmer of hope appeared. The sky was no longer black, but grey. It transitioned into a blue haze, casting light onto the faces of her near neighbours. The first she'd been able to see since departing the shores of Izmir.

To her left, she noticed a small girl. No more than seven. An angelic face. A shivering body swallowed up by her life jacket. She leaned into an ageing woman who looked too old to be her mother. They both appeared Arab.

From somewhere in the crowd, Amira heard a mention of land, spoken in her own tongue.

Cries from the bow of the dinghy confirmed it.

Everyone seemed to get the message. Amira saw smiles

on faces. Felt her own mouth crease, the sickness in her stomach suspended for a precious moment. A man at the front yelled something about a beach. It was close. Less than a mile, another said.

Less than a mile. The waves would grow smaller. The dinghy would run ashore with the gentle, fizzing surf. Amira would step into the turtle-blue shallows. Dust her feet with the golden sands of whichever beach they landed on.

She would feel her stomach settle on solid ground. Her energy return. Then would come food, water, sunny skies . . . Amira snapped awake from her daydream.

A large wave hit with shuddering force. Seawater rained ice-cold over her head. She felt the wave roll underneath the dinghy. The bow rising steep to the left.

The first passengers fell off the side. Legs and feet disappearing into the water. The dinghy tipped steeper, almost ninety degrees. People panicked and screamed.

Another wave pounded the small craft. Amira slid to her left, swamped in a giant tangle of scrambling bodies.

She couldn't hold on. No one could. There was nothing—and no one—left to hold onto.

Chapter 2

Going straight is tougher than it looks, especially during lunch and dinner service. I've been waiting tables at Gastronomy for a week. And I still haven't figured out how to work the card machine.

But I can't complain. In fact, I'm pretty damn lucky.

I only got the job because I was walking down the street when the previous waiter stormed out. He quit on the spot right in front of me. Threw his apron down on the pavement.

I picked it up and stepped inside. Asked the owner, Chef Dubois, if he needed a hand. I lied about my experience and he was desperate.

So I got the job.

Well, a week's trial at least. And I've been working my arse off ever since, taking every shift the little Parisian bastard will throw at me.

Up until this gig, finding work was impossible.

My C.V. is basically a sheet of paper with a name on it. I've got no qualifications. No education. You can't exactly put enforcer work down in your employment history. And what am I supposed to put under skills? Breaking legs? Hanging people off buildings? Negotiating wholesale drug deals? No, you can't put any of that down.

And I doubt doing metalwork in Strangeways prison counts as a job.

So when Dubois bollocks me yet again in the kitchen, I take it on the chin.

"Pointer," he says, "table two are still waiting on their wine."

Shit, I forgot.

"Yes, chef," I say, sliding a pair of empty plates onto a counter. "On it, Chef."

"You're still on trial Pointer," he reminds me as I fly back out of the swing doors.

Yeah, the guy's got me by the balls.

I grab table two's bottle of wine off the bar top and weave through the packed restaurant.

My name's Pointer, for now. Trev Pointer. Or Trevor James Pointer, according to my new passport. Not that Dubois has a clue who I am, but it's best to be careful. Keep my head down. Don't give the police or Rudenko's mob a sniff of my whereabouts.

I sort table two out with the wine and hurry over to another table where a young kid is playing with his ice cream. He's got a haystack of blonde hair and a look in his eye that says trouble. While mum and dad deal with a wailing tot, he scoops some ice cream on the end of a spoon and flicks it at me. Next thing I know, I've got caramel vanilla running down my nose. I smile and wipe it off. He flicks some more. It splats on my cheek. Again, I wipe it off. I'd like to teach the bleeder some manners. But I laugh and ruffle his hair. As I lean over the table and gather the dirty dishes, he tips the melted remains of the ice cream into my apron pocket.

"Oh Ollie, don't do that," his mum says half-hearted.

"It's alright," I say. "Boys will be boys."

I walk away with a stack of dishes, ice cream dribbling down the front of my pants.

Dubois is on me in a flash. "Pointer, you're dripping all over my floor."

The guy is worse than the cops, with his big black quiff and beady little eyes watching your every move. At five-six, he's almost a foot shorter than me. I could knock him into the ground with one thump of my fist, but you can't do that in the real world. The rules are different. The bullies are the little men with a string if letters after their name.

Besides, I'm not that man any more. It's my new mantra.

"Sorry, chef," I say, biting my tongue. "I'll get a mop."

I tell you one thing, ice creaming a man's pants would *not* stand in the underworld.

* * *

The rush continues for the rest of the evening. Being on my feet all day is a shock to the system. In my old profession, there was a lot of sitting around. In cars, bars, mafia fronts— either waiting for the phone to ring or something to happen. And just when it's quietening down in the restaurant, a hen party bundle their way in late. A dozen forty-something women in pink t-shirts and tutus. One of them wearing a tiara. Another carrying a giant inflatable dick. They play merry hell with me. Slapping me on the arse, talking dirty.

I play along with a smile. Lift the bride-to-be down when she gets up and dances on the table. Laugh at their mucky jokes and try and keep 'em quiet with food and wine. They tip me well and leave. I lock the restaurant door behind them. Wipe the tables down with Piotr, a spotty young kid with shaved blonde hair and glasses. We stack the chairs upside down on the tables. I head into the kitchen to grab a broom from the store cupboard.

The kitchen is empty of cooks. Only Dubois still here. He's stood by the back fire exit door with two burly blokes in dark suits. One in navy, the other in black. Both with white, open-neck shirts underneath. They're short on hair, but big on gold jewellery. Ugly too, like ex-boxers.

Dubois hands over a brown envelope full of cash.

The man in a navy suit rifles through the notes with a finger. "You're two hundred short," he says, in a deep cockney voice.

"It's the usual amount," Dubois says.

"The premium's gone up," the bloke in black says. "Twenty percent."

"Come on," Dubois says. "This is all I've got—"

"Relax, Franky baby," the guy says, tapping a hand against Dubois' cheek. "We'll get it off you next month."

I open a utility cupboard and pull out the broom. I can't help staring.

The guy in navy glances over. "What are you looking at, Tinker Bell?"

Dubois turns. Waves me away.

I close the cupboard and walk out of the kitchen. The two men eyeball me all the way out of the door.

Chapter 3

Before she could take a breath, a second large wave dumped Amira and the others into the sea. Under the water, it was a chaotic tumble of arms and legs and terrified faces, kicking and fighting for space, for air, for life. Amira popped out onto the surface. A large, diagonal wave rolled towards her at speed. A deep blue juggernaut that picked her up and carried her backwards. Saltwater stung the inside of her nostrils. She swallowed a mouthful and gasped for air in the freezing Aegean.

Some refugees made for shore—chopping their way through a three-quarter mile swim. Others flailed and thrashed, going nowhere but down.

The life jackets were not up to the task. Amira was sure hers was faulty—only half inflated—and hers wasn't the only one.

Amira's instinct was to kick for dry land, but she couldn't help looking for that little girl and her ageing relative. She didn't see the older woman, but she did see the girl. Twenty metres to her right, caught in a mess of panicking bodies.

The girl screamed for help between gulps of water, unable to stay afloat. A large, frantic man dragged her down with him, her lifejacket ripped from her tiny body.

Amira front-crawled towards the girl, attempting to cut through the crowd. But it was useless. A wall of wheeling limbs slapped into her head and shoulders. She pulled away and hurried to unfasten the string tie around her lifejacket.

Her hands trembling underwater, Amira loosened the tie. She pulled her lifejacket over her head and let it float away. She wrestled herself out of her soaking black coat, seeing the girl forced under as another large wave rolled in.

Amira took a deep breath.

Before the wave could carry her further from the girl, she ducked under the surface, diving a metre down. Moving free from the constraints of her lifejacket, she kicked beneath the swimmers.

Eyes open, Amira saw the girl slip below the surface, her stick thin legs kicking in vain.

She swam hard towards the girl. Caught her as she dropped deeper and made for the surface. They emerged together into a clear stretch of water. The girl cried for her grandmother, coughing up water. Amira held her close and looked around. Saw only people heading towards shore. She turned again. The capsized dinghy rushed towards them. Amira told the girl to take a deep breath. She pushed the child's head under the water and followed her down.

The dinghy drifted overhead like a dead whale. Amira saw lifeless bodies caught beneath the capsized boat. She covered the girl's eyes until the dinghy passed by. She dragged the girl to the surface once more. They took a collective breath.

"We have to swim," Amira said, turning onto her back and holding the girl above the water. "Help me," she said, her teeth chattering.

Together they swam backwards towards the shore, riding the tide. The current was merciful, taking them in to a small beach, rather than the rocks on either side of the cove.

As they reached the shallows, the water grew warmer. The sun rose higher in the sky. Amira felt her shoulder blades drag against the sand below the water. Yet the surf hit the pair hard as waves rushed in, one on top of the other.

Amira fought to her feet, pulling the girl up. The waves smashed into her legs, already shaky from the swim. She fought against the tide, carrying the girl and wading onto the beach.

Every step sapped more of her strength, the wet sand like glue, sucking at her feet. Exhausted and frozen, her sickness had abated the moment the dinghy capsized. Amira dropped to the dry, fine sand further up the beach. She lay next to the girl and looked along the shore. A pile of lifejackets discarded. Some of the surviving passengers already moving on. Others sitting with heads in hands, or screaming out to sea, mourning lost loved ones.

The girl sobbed gentle tears, curled in a shivering ball. "Grandma . . . Where is Grandma?"

Amira sat up. She put an arm around the girl's shoulders, holding her close. "Your grandma is gone," Amira said. "I'm sorry."

The girl cried into the pink shirt stuck to Amira's goose-pimpled skin.

"We have to go," Amira said, hoisting the girl to her feet against her will.

The child wept and wailed, hysterical, fighting to collapse to the floor.

Amira wouldn't let her. She shook her by both arms, raising her voice. *"We live with what we have,"* Amira said, then quieter as the girl calmed down. "Together, agreed?"

The girl looked into Amira's eyes. Hair stuck wet to her head and neck. She shivered as if absorbing electric currents. Yet she nodded in agreement.

"I won't leave you," Amira said, putting a palm to the girl's face. "I promise."

Hand in hand, they staggered in the footsteps of the others, coating their feet in dry, fine sand. The line of survivors snaked upwards, between the rocks of wherever it was they'd landed. The sun shone on their backs. It also twinkled off the frothing shallows of the cove, where dead bodies and dinghy washed ashore.

Chapter 4

The next day, I'm working another long shift, starting with lunch. It's quiet. A few business types.

Dubois sees his place as a swanky high-end French bistro. The truth is it's a couple of rungs below. The British version of French cuisine. Steak, garlic bread and triple cooked fries the most popular things on the menu. Still, the food is good here. There's a few times I've sampled the leftovers with the others. But so far, I've resisted the urge to nick one of those cheese tarts, hot off the tray. And I'm only borrowing one of the spare forks I found lying around on a worktop. No, if I'm gonna play it straight, might as well go the whole hog.

As we hit two in the afternoon, the restaurant goes dead. Dubois leaves his assistant chef in charge of the kitchen. Piotr punches out for the day.

I'm sitting at the bar at the back of the restaurant, when in walk those two heavies stiffing Dubois for cash. They take a seat in the middle of the restaurant, wearing the same suits as the night before. The one in black waves me to their table. I grab a couple of menus off the bar and carry them over.

I greet them as normal. "Welcome to Gastronomy. Can I get you something to drink?"

I hand over the menus. They throw 'em aside.

"Two pints of whatever Frog lager you've got on tap," the one in black says.

"And two garlic breads to start," the guy in navy says. "The ones with the melted cheese."

"Coming right up," I say, putting on a smile.

I return with their pints. Dubois' second in command knocks up a couple of garlic pizza breads.

I take 'em over. "Here you go gentlemen. Enjoy."

As I clear another table, I see 'em watching me. Talking as they demolish their food. As if they're talking about me.

I act like I don't notice. The last thing I want is to get involved with a pair of local hoods. Instead, I clear their plates, get 'em fresh pints and take their order for steak and fries. I return to the table with their mains. I turn to leave 'em to it.

"Hang on mate," the one in black says. "Don't I recognise you?"

"Uh-uh. Don't think so."

"You look familiar," the one in navy says. "Where are you from?"

"Here and there," I say.

"Sounds like a northern accent to me," the guy in the black says. "What you reckon, Gaz?"

"Yeah," Gaz says, "Manchester, I'd say, Daz."

Gaz eats his fries with his fingers. "You hear about what happened up there with that Rudenko geezer? I heard one of his own men put him away."

"Ah, yeah," Daz says, cutting into his steak. "Fella was supposed to pop a witness. But he helped the little shit instead. Fucked Rudenko over. Can you believe that?"

I stand there and keep quiet.

"So you heard about it or what?" Gaz asks me.

"No pal," I say. "I've not been back there for years."

"Is that right?" Daz says, supping on his pint. "Then you also won't have heard about the price on the geezer's head."

"Sorry gents," I say, "but what's this gotta do with me?"

"Just making conversation," Gaz says. "That a crime, is it?"

I fake a smile. "Course not. Enjoy your mains."

I walk away, watch them from the kitchens. By the time I return to clear their plates, Dubois is back and they're up on their feet.

I head over with the bill in hand, about to remind 'em they've not paid. I feel a feather-grip on my forearm. Dubois takes the bill off me and rips it in two. Shakes his head.

Daz turns as they head out the door. "Be seeing you," he says to me.

* * *

It's chaos in the kitchens. There's a works party—got the whole place booked out and two cooks haven't turned up. Which means I'm doubling up for the night. Scrubbing pots. Taking things out of the ovens.

I'm a fish out of water in the kitchen. My experience limited to holding faces over stoves. Hitting a bloke over the head with a wok. Chopping off a mobster's finger with a meat knife.

As I dash out of the restaurant into the kitchens, I smell something burning.

Shit, the garlic bread.

I fling an oven door open. Black smoke pours out. The pizza-shaped dough looks like it took a hit from an RPG.

I slide the smouldering black wreck in the bin and grab a fresh bread off the counter. I wave the smoke out of the oven with a towel and slide the replacement dough inside.

I set the timer and take a full-scale assault from Pepe Le Pew.

"Pointer you imbecile, you were supposed to be watching that!" He shouts as he stirs a sauce in a pan.

"I can't be in two places at once," I say.

"You'll be any fucking thing I tell you," says Dubois, pointing to the cremated garlic bread, sticking out of the bin. "Now get that monstrosity out of my kitchen. The smell offends me."

"Yes, chef," I say, grabbing two overflowing bins and heading to the fire exit.

"And make it quick," Dubois says. "We're behind as it is."

I push open the fire exit door and head into the alleyway. Feel the cool air on my face. Breathe in the smell of piss.

Night has already fallen. I turn left and carry the bins towards their big blue and orange counterparts. I throw the lid open on the nearest one and get a lungful of something rotten. A raw chicken turning into a sea of maggots.

I empty the first one in. Then the second. As I'm closing the lid on the larger bin, I notice a car driving up the alley.

The driver dips the headlights. I blink the spots from my eyes. Two men climb out and walk around the front of the car. Mere shadows until they break into the light spilling out from the kitchens.

Oh great, it's Gaz and Daz.

Gaz has a baseball bat and Daz a tyre iron.

"Evening lads," I say.

"Get in the car," says Gaz.

"You what?"

"You heard," Daz says. "Get in the fucking car."

"But I've got a garlic bread in the oven."

"I don't care if you've got the Queen's birthday cake in there," Gaz says. "In the fucking motor, now."

I hear Dubois shouting me in from the kitchens. Yelling at me to get my arse back inside.

I put down the bins. "Look, what's this all about chaps?"

"You know what," Gaz says.

"Ah, the Manchester thing," I say. "News travels, eh?"

"There's a pretty penny on your head, sunshine," Daz says. "Lucky for you, Rudenko's boys want you alive."

"And did they happen to tell you who I am?"

"Just that you're a fucking turncoat," Gaz says. "Thought we recognised you last night. Your ugly mug's doing the rounds on a text."

"I see . . . Well, before we do this, do you mind if I take my apron off?"

Chapter 5

The Greek sun had dried their ragged clothes, but night brought the cold once again. They'd followed the other survivors into a camp on the edge of Agios Andreas. It was a mess of thin, pale blue tents—each one overcrowded and pegged into a mud floor.

White marquees set up around the perimeter were empty, abandoned. Amira and the young girl had wandered them all in search of aid. Only dusty tables and litter remained.

At least water was available through a running tap. They waited in line for their turn, filling up a couple of large plastic bottles found on the floor of a marquee. They warmed themselves in front of a deserted fire in a steel bin stuffed with card, paper, rags and twigs.

The young girl's name was Rima. She cried for her grandmother, her mother, her father—but soon fell asleep. As Amira began to drift, she saw three figures approach, beyond the crackle and snap of the fire. They moved as if searching for someone. Or something.

They were men of different races. Languid, gaunt, hollow-eyed in the uplight of the fire. Amira kept her head down and averted her gaze. After a moment or two, she glanced up again. They were staring her way. They split and approached around the fire. Amira tensed. Rima stirred. Amira realised she was squeezing the young girl's arm.

The men crouched either side.

"Hey," one said. Arabic. "How are you?"

"Okay," Amira said.

"Can we get you anything?"

One of the men—an African—said something in his own language.

His Arab friend nodded, as if he understood. "You don't have to sleep out here. We have a tent."

"Who are you?" Amira asked.

"Relax," the man said. "We're site security—unofficial—we make sure everyone's looked after."

Amira looked from one man to another. They smiled and nodded.

"The fire won't last all night," the man continued. "Come and sleep in our tent."

Amira eyed each of the men again. "No thank you," she said. "We'll be fine. We've got more card we can throw on."

The man doing the talking put a hand on Amira's shoulder. "Don't be silly. Come with us."

Amira shook off his hand. She pulled Rima in close. "Thank you, but we're fine as we are."

The men conferred. The African ran a finger down Amira's left cheek. She pulled away again, onto her feet. She dragged a stirring Rima up with her. The men jumped up and surrounded them. Rima asked what was happening, her voice sleepy.

"Nothing," the Arab man said. "We're just talking to your mother."

"Come on Rima," Amira said, "we're going."

"No, stay," the Arab man said. "We insist."

The three men grabbed at Amira. She felt a hand on her right breast. Another on her buttocks. She slapped them away, but the men were getting rough. Pushing her around. Amira shouted for help.

The African attempted to muffle her cries. She bit into his hand. It tasted of diseased sweat. She seized a plank of wood jutting out of the fire. She waved it left to right at the men, the end of the plank in flames.

"Get away," Amira said.

The men regrouped in front of her. They advanced slow. Amira warded them off, but they kept coming. Lunging. Seeming to enjoy the challenge.

Amira kicked the bin over in front of them. The fire spilled out and caught the men by surprise.

She took Rima by the hand and ran. The fire caught on a pile of cardboard and flared, buying them a head start.

They stumbled through the tents, struggling to see in the dark. The ground uneven.

Amira glanced over her shoulder. The men were like phantom shadows chasing them through the camp. As she turned her attention to the space ahead, her foot caught on a tent rope pegged into the ground. The rope twanged and snapped. Amira hit the ground hard, Rima tumbling with her.

The men closed in.

"Come on," Rima said, helping Amira to her feet.

The two of them ran on, into the nearest abandoned marquee. Amira felt her lungs burn. She slowed to a stop to catch her breath. Rima was about to say something. Amira put a hand over her mouth and listened. She heard the men shouting to each other. They'd split up, entering the marquee from opposite ends, cutting off any means of escape.

Amira attempted to calm her spiralling mind. She looked around her in the gloom. Saw a giant pile of rubbish to their right—bottles, rags, bandages and flattened boxes. "Here," she whispered to Rima, leading her to the mountain of flotsam.

"What are you doing?" Rima whispered.

"We're playing hide and seek," Amira said, creating a space at the base of the pile. She pulled Rima down with her into the rubbish. She dragged a used bed sheet and a large flattened cardboard box over their bodies.

"I like hide and seek," Rima said.

"Me too," Amira said, "But we need to be quiet as mice. Okay?"

"Okay," Rima said.

Amira held her own breath, her hand over Rima's mouth. They huddled tight as the men approached. Shouts from afar shrinking into close conversation.

"No one saw her?" the Arab man said. "Shit, I got to have

that bitch. Keep looking. I need to piss."

Amira heard the man unzip his fly. A stream of urine pattered against the opposite side of the cardboard. The Arab sighed in relief.

The stream petered out. A sharp zipping sound as the man did up his fly. The soles of his trainers shuffling away.

Fortunately for Amira and Rima, the cardboard was thick, folded into three layers. The urine hadn't soaked through. Amira kicked it away, the smell of ammonia overpowering. She flung the bed sheet aside and told Rima to stay put. Amira edged around the rubbish pile. She looked both ways. The men were gone. She helped Rima to her feet, letting out her breath. "Come on," Amira said.

"Where are we going?" Rima asked, taking her hand.

"Anywhere but here," Amira said.

Chapter 6

I untie the apron from around the small of my back.

"Ooh, careful Daz," says Gaz. "He's taking his pinny off."

The boys laugh. They go loose. I lift the apron over the top of my head, I toss it in Daz's face. It buys me a split second. I barge him onto the bonnet of their Jag saloon.

Gaz reacts, swinging his bat. I pick up a bin and use it as a shield. The bin spins out of one hand, but I get both on the bat handle. We wrestle for control. Daz is up off the bonnet. I rotate the bat and catch him in the face. He drops to the ground. The tyre iron clangs against the concrete. I run Gaz backwards and slam him into the nearest brick wall. I drive a knee into his ribs. He doubles over. I ram his hand against the wall and he lets go of the bat. Before I can use it, he rugby tackles me to the ground.

It takes me by surprise. I drop the bat and it rolls off under the car.

I kick Gaz in the face. Roll away as Daz tries to smash my skull with the tyre iron.

It connects with the alley floor.

I pick up the other bin and bring it down over Daz's head. It wedges tight around his shoulders. He drops the tyre iron and stumbles blind. I shoulder charge him to the floor.

As Gaz comes back at me, I greet him with a fist to the jaw. He wobbles. I grab the collar of his blazer and pound him a few more times. His face is a bloody mess. I ram his head into the wall again. Gravity lends a hand and he lands face-first in a bag of rubbish. It splits in two, painting his face in thrown-out spaghetti.

Meanwhile, Daz wanders in circles, trying to prise the bin off his upper body. I realise the engine of the Jag is still running. I climb behind the wheel and put it in first.

Daz forces the bin off his head in time to blink into the headlights.

I floor the accelerator and drive straight into the bastard.

He pops off the bonnet and rolls along the alley. Nothing fatal, but enough to finish him off.

I climb out of the Jag and approach Gaz. I dig around in his pockets. Find his phone. He hasn't bothered code-locking the thing. A quick search through his texts reveals an old police mugshot of me. It says: *Alive. £20k. Whereabouts unknown.*

Not for much longer. Not when these two clowns wake up and word spreads.

Then I'll have all kinds of dickheads showing up at Dubois' door.

And I really needed this bloody job.

I gather the bins and double-back through the kitchen

door. Dubois is close to boiling point. I open the oven door and get a face full of smoke.

Bollocks. I burnt the garlic bread again.

Chapter 7

More fires lit in bins had warmed their hands as they passed into Macedonia. Train rides had carried them to Serbia. Now, deserted tracks guided Amira and Rima to the Hungarian border.

Rima was tough. Didn't complain about the blisters on her feet or the nasty cough on her chest.

But she was getting worse. Her temperature high. Her body weak. Her skin turning pale.

Traipsing in a long line of refugees, Amira didn't have to be a doctor to know Rima needed urgent medical care. The best she could do was keep her warm. A discarded blue coat had helped. It was several sizes too big. The sleeves flapped long over Rima's hands. The tail of the coat extended down to her ankles. But Rima loved it.

Amira herself had found a red woollen sweater caught in a prickly bush. She'd bloodied her fingers prising it off the thorns.

Mile after mile they trudged, Rima receiving a piggy-back ride for a few of them, from a man travelling on his own.

Finally, the border came into sight. It wasn't pretty. A tall fence with barbed wire at the top. Armed guards in dark-blue uniforms, pale-blue hygiene masks strapped around their faces.

The line of refugees came to a grinding halt. Then a slow shuffle into a camp. A muddy field where they stood in rows, waiting to be processed.

Amira jostled her way to the front with Rima. She spoke in English to the guards, who stood in front of another fence.

Behind the fence was a train station platform and a small car park. Amira noticed a white coach loading up with refugees.

Most of the guards didn't understand English. But one did. A blonde man with a large nose and narrow eyes. He pulled his mask down to talk.

"What's happening?" Amira asked.

"You will be put on train. Or bus," the guard said. "Taken to Austrian border."

"When?"

"Soon as possible," the guard said. "Please, in line."

"How long do we wait?" Amira asked.

"A day," the guard said. "Or two."

"The girl is sick. She won't last out here. Can't you do something? Get her some help?"

"Sorry," the guard said. "Please, in line."

So they waited. On their feet. On the seat of their pants. Rima lay with her head on Amira's chest.

As the night drew in, some refugees had small tents they were able to put up. Large sodium lights made it harder to sleep, but easier for the guards to watch over the crowd.

The field was filling up with refugees. Dozens by the hour. Amira huddled close to the girl, as much for her own warmth as Rima's.

Drifting in and out of nightmares, she felt a hand on her shoulder. A face in the dark. The man who'd given Rima a piggy back. Rangy and lean, with deep, dark circles under his eyes.

Amira jumped. *"Get away."*

"No, it's okay," the man said in a soft voice. "I can get you on the coach. There's one leaving soon. But you have to pay."

"To Austria?" Amira asked.

"To Germany," the man said with a smile. "That's where you're headed, right?"

Amira's eyes lit up. Help for Rima and the promise of Germany, where she had family. The only family she had left. The only dream to cling to. "How much?" she asked.

"A thousand each. You have it?"

"Yes, I have it."

"Then come, follow me."

Amira shook Rima awake. The girl could barely raise an eyelid.

"Here," the man said, scooping Rima up in his arms.

Amira rose to her feet, her backside sodden with cold, wet mud. She followed the man through the sleeping crowds—a sea of bodies huddling for warmth. A broken rainbow of tents dotted between.

The guard who spoke English opened a gate on the fence

and let them through, looking neither of them in the eye. They walked across a dark stretch of unlit concrete behind the railway platform. To a waiting coach. Plain white. Its engine ticking over. A shadowy figure stood at the open door at the front. He had a clipboard and a leather money bag strapped around his front. A long, black coat open at the front and a thick grey scarf high around his neck.

He looked like he might be local to Amira, though in the low light spilling out from the coach, she couldn't tell.

"You got money?" the man asked.

"Yes," Amira said, unbuttoning her trousers at the waist. She unzipped the clear plastic pouch she'd had the good sense to stitch into her trousers. It was waterproof and hidden from sight. She counted her way through a wedge of notes before pulling out the required amount. "Germany, yes?" she asked.

The man shook his head. "Netherlands."

Amira held onto the money. "But you said Germany."

"That's what he told me," the man travelling with her said.

"There's been a change of plan," the man in the coat and scarf said. "The coach is leaving now. You're either on it or you're not."

Amira looked at Rima. She handed over the money.

The man counted it out again and stuffed it inside his own money bag. "That pays for you," he said. "What about the child?"

"She's just a kid," the man helping Amira said.

"Payment is for seat, not size of person."

"I've only got two hundred," Amira said, hoping the lie would stick.

The man humphed and thought it over. "Okay, two hundred."

Amira handed over the extra fare. The man took the money and directed them on-board the coach.

The driver was a small bald man in a black fleece and jeans. He handed Amira three litre-bottles of water from a torn open pack at the front of the coach. He reached inside a tatty carrier bag and handed over the same number of energy bars. He did it without a hint of warmth. Amira wasn't complaining. She thanked the driver and walked along the aisle. The coach was only half full. Not everyone had the savings to spend on a fast-track journey to western Europe.

The man helping Amira laid Rima out on a window seat halfway down the aisle. Amira thanked him and took the seat next to her; the man settling in across from them. Amira removed Rima's coat. She opened it out and flung it over the pair of them. They sat close together, as if they were mother and daughter.

The coach doors folded closed. The air brakes hissed and the driver revved the diesel engine hard. The coach set off across the car park. The heaters came on overhead. Amira closed her eyes and dreamed of a better life.

Chapter 8

I sleep on it for the night.

When I wake up, I'm still of the same opinion.

It's not safe for me, or the rest of the Gastronomy staff. Not even the customers.

Now the word's out about where I work, Gaz and Daz'll be just the appetiser.

So I head into work as usual. Only I'm not there long.

"I can't work here anymore, Mr Dubois."

Dubois looks up from sampling a pan of soup he's working on. He pulls his face. "Too much salt," he says to himself.

"Mr Dubois?"

He tastes the soup again. "Your trial's up tomorrow," he says. "I was going to fire you anyway."

"Oh," I say, disappointed. It would have been nice to get the job, even if I can't accept it. "You want me to work the rest of the day?"

"No," Dubois says, his tongue as sharp as his lemon tart. "I've lined up someone else."

I linger on the spot as he adds a pinch of salt to the soup. "Uh, what about my wages?"

"Payment at the end of the week," he says. "I'll transfer it then."

"Okay," I say, turning to leave. I stop with a hand on the kitchen door. "Those dickheads who charge you protection money . . . You won't have to pay 'em anymore."

Dubois pauses, the spoon an inch from his lips. He lowers it into the pan. "What do you mean?"

"I had a word with 'em."

Dubois can't seem to wrap his head around the fact.

"You're welcome," I say, on my way out of the door.

With my working day over by noon, I head for the nearest pub. The closest affordable boozer to Gastronomy is The Old Ship. A ten minute stomp down a smog-filled high street. I head inside. It's a traditional place. Musty and grim. A flashing fruit machine in the corner and a maroon pool table towards the far end. The pub smells of stale ales and cigarettes smoked before the ban. The kind of hole only alcoholics and old men with skinny dogs frequent during the day.

I slide onto a bar stool and take out my phone as it rings. It's a video call from Cassie.

She pops up on the screen, sat on some stone steps. Like she's outside a library or something. "Hey, Dad," she says, a strand of blonde hair escaping from a green wooly hat.

"Hi sweetheart. How's uni?"

"Oh, uni's okay," she says. "You not working today?"

"I'm working four till eleven," I say, scratching the back of my neck.

"What's wrong with your hand?"

"What do you mean?"

"It looks bruised or something."

I study the redness on my knuckles, courtesy of Gaz's face.

"Don't tell me you've been fighting again."

"Oh, I caught my hand on one of the ovens . . . You know your old man. Clumsy bastard, aren't I?" I look again at Cassie's surroundings. "Where are you? Why aren't you in lectures?"

"It's reading week," she says.

"What's that when it's at home?"

"It's kind of like a week off. I've read all the books already."

"So just chillin', huh?"

Cassie rolls her eyes the way her mother does. "Please don't use words like *chillin'*, Dad."

"Oh sorry, I'll keep it real, shall I?"

"You're so last century," she says.

"Who you talking to?" I hear a young guy say, off-camera.

"Just my Dad," Cassie says.

"Who's that?" I ask, feeling my heckles rise. "You got a boyfriend?"

"No, Dad. Don't flip out. It's just Sam."

"Just Sam, eh? Well what are you and *Just Sam* up to?"

"We're at a protest."

"Another one? What's it about this time?"

"Fur," Cassie says. "They're having a fashion show at the

art gallery. Some of it's real. It's disgraceful, Dad."

"Well the animals won't miss it," I say. "They're dead, aren't they?"

"They don't just wait for them to die, Dad. They kill them for it . . . Don't you know anything?"

"I wish you'd stop all this protesting bollocks, you're gonna get yourself in trouble."

"Yeah, so?"

"So I don't want you having a criminal record."

"Dad, I'm not gonna—"

"No, listen to me Cass. The pigs—I mean, these riot police are mean bastards. They'll baton you as soon as look at you."

"There's not gonna be a riot, Dad. It's a peaceful protest. There's three of us chained to a gatepost, that's all."

I shake my head. "Well as long as it's legal."

"Sam studies law. It's legal, isn't it Sam?"

"It is?" I hear Sam say. "I mean, it is. Yes, perfectly."

"Look, I've gotta go," Cassie says. "Just wanted to check up on you. Make sure you're okay."

"Let me do the worrying, sweetheart. Stay out of trouble."

As we end the call, a fat, bald man appears behind the brass-railed bar. He wears an England football shirt, his belly sticking out over the waist of his jeans. "Sorry mate, I was changing the barrel. What can I get you?"

I look across the taps. A range of solid ales. None of that fancy designer nonsense.

"Pint of lager, please."

The landlord picks up a glass and pulls me a pint. He rests it on the bar and tells me the damage.

"Five quid a pint?" I say, counting my coins. "Jam on toast again tonight."

The landlord shrugs and rubs a pint glass dry with a towel.

"London prices," says a man with an East End accent. He takes the stool next to me. Leather jacket and jeans. Sandy hair and a cocky grin. "You're not up north now, you tight fucker."

I fix him with a stare.

He stares back. A pint of Guinness and a folded-up paper in front of him. "Northern monkey," he says, slurping the head off his pint.

"Soft southern shit," I say, sipping my cold pint of lager.

The landlord takes a step back from the bar, like there's gonna be a rumble.

Chris Randall puts down his pint and breaks into laughter. He rises off his stool. Me off mine. We shake hands. I slap him on the arm.

"Breaker, what the hell are you doing here?" he says.

"Having a pint. What does it look like?"

"Been around long?" he asks.

"About a month."

"You should have said."

"Thought you were still in the nick, Chris."

"Got out a year ago," Randall says. "Good behaviour . . . So what brings you down here? You settling a score for someone?"

"Nah, I'm done with all that. Playing it straight."

Randall laughs. Sups on his pint. Double-takes. "Seriously?"

"Uh-huh."

"So what are you doing instead?"

"Anything that'll pay the rent. As long as it's honest, I don't mind."

Randall puts down his pint and shakes his head. "Charlie Cobb, underworld hard-man and legendary fixer, working for a living."

"Well, I was until about half an hour ago."

Randall pauses. Looks at me like he's thinking. "How straight is the path, exactly?"

"What's that mean?"

Randall lowers his voice. Leans in to me. "I've got this job."

"It's not waiting on tables, is it?"

Randall laughs into his pint. "God, no."

"Hang on Chris," I say, finding myself a little too interested. "I don't wanna know."

"It's nothing heavy."

"Sorry pal," I say.

"It's only fake merch, Charlie."

"I don't care if it's fake snow. I don't wanna handle anything iffy,"

"You won't be handling anything. You won't even see it. I'm after a driver, that's all."

"Where from?"

"Ramsgate. You pick up the truck in port, pre-loaded and ready to rock. All you have to do is drive it back to the big smoke."

"Why do you need it driving out from there?"

"Because the arsehole I hired decided to have a drink on the ferry from Belgium. Only he can't handle his booze, can he? So he gets pissed up, starts a fight and does a runner when he hits port. I get a call from the ferry company telling me the truck's parked up in fucking Ramsgate."

"And the driver?"

Chris shakes his head. "Fuck knows, mate . . ." Point is, I can't get another driver who knows how to handle a truck. So the merch is sat there by the side of the coast road. And I've made promises, you know?"

"I see your problem," I say, sinking the rest of my pint. "How much?"

"A lot more than being a waiter pays. And if it works out, you can have the drunken bastard's routes."

"I dunno," I say. "I swore I wouldn't do anything dodgy."

"Come on, Breaker. Most of it's tat sold by eBay mums. You'll be putting food in the mouths of little kiddies. It'd be a crime not to."

Randall's always been a persuasive guy. The slick salesman at the centre of everything. The only thing he ever handled was the money. You do the work. He takes his cut. The rest goes to whoever's paying for the job.

But he's one of the good guys. I'd trust him with my life—matter of fact, I have, on more than one occasion.

Randall takes a biro from inside his jacket and scribbles a phone number on his newspaper. He tears it off at the corner and hands it over.

I pocket the number and push my empty pint glass across

the bar top. I stand off my stool and pat him on the shoulder. "Good seeing you mate. I'll think about it."

Randall raises his half empty pint glass. "Don't think too long."

Chapter 9

The coach rumbled on. An endless stretch of motorways, dual carriageways and border crossings. Amira had exchanged some of her remaining life savings for euros in Turkey. She'd spent a small amount of them on blankets, water, pre-packed sandwiches and fruit for her and Rima.

But Rima had stopped eating. She was restless, grouchy, her skin clammy with sweat. Her cough getting worse. All Amira could do was coax her to drink, keep her warm and nurse her to sleep.

She offered her spare food to the man who'd helped them on-board. His name was Malik. He was a former soldier from Afghanistan. He'd returned to his civilian role of physicist, only to lose his job after the bombing of his lab. He had no home, job or family. But enough money to pay for passage to a fresh start in Europe. He told Amira he hoped to become a scientist again once he found his feet. Perhaps at a university.

After telling Amira his story and finishing his sandwiches, Malik fell asleep. Amira yawned and rolled out her neck. She'd made it through another night, to see the sun rise in the East.

The coach had passed through Hungary into Austria. The scenery had changed. Now came mountains and valleys. Rolling carpets of green, snaking blue rivers and swathes of dense, dark forest.

Amira couldn't believe her eyes. She felt excited for the first time. This was *really* happening. This was the Europe she'd dreamed of. The roads were free of holes. The buildings and tunnels in one, well-maintained piece. The sky was crisp and blue: not a missile or plume of mushrooming smoke in sight.

And flying past the coach, the occasional Mercedes, Audi and BMW. Not caked in dust or rubble, but polished to a gleam, the sun winking off alloy rims and chrome badges.

Amira nudged Rima awake and pointed out of the window. "Look Rima. Look at how beautiful it is. We're almost there."

A smile flickered on Rima's face like a bulb with a loose connection. She took in the view: the snowy mountain peaks and wispy white clouds casting shadows over the fields. Rima let out a weak gasp. "This is Germany?"

"No, Austria," Amira said. "But not long now."

Rima remained awake, eyes glued to the scenery. Amira held back the news about the Netherlands. She didn't want to confuse the girl in her weakened state

On towards Germany the coach continued. Only hour-long sleep breaks for the driver punctuated the onward movement.

Amira wanted to stay awake for the rest of the journey.

To see Germany, the Netherlands too. She'd heard there were fields of tulips and windmills. What a sight that would be . . . Yet she could hang on no longer. Her eyelids closed as the coach headed north east.

* * *

By the time she opened them again, she heard an argument at the front of the coach. It was Malik, remonstrating with the driver. The other passengers watching on and murmuring to each other.

Amira looked out of the window. The coach was on another stretch of motorway. The road signs in a different colour and language to that of the German autobahn.

She checked on Rima. She was shivering in her sleep. Her temperature higher than ever. Amira thought she'd been getting better, yet she appeared to be getting worse. She eased Rima's head off her bosom. The sleepy young girl repositioned herself against the window curtain.

Amira got to her feet, her body stiff and aching. She stretched out her lower back and shook out her legs. She made her way to the front of the coach, hands on headrests to keep her upright.

Malik was irate. He turned to Amira. "Now he says we're not going to the Netherlands."

"What?" Amira said, still sleepy.

"Change of plan," the driver said, as if it was the official line that killed all arguments.

"I don't understand," Amira said. "What do you mean? Where are we?"

"Belgium," Malik said. "We're in Belgium."

"What are we doing in Belgium?"

"Change of plan," the driver repeated.

"What are we going to do here?" Amira said. "We were promised—"

"I only drive bus," the driver said. "They phone me and tell me to reroute. So I reroute."

"Who told you?" Malik asked.

"The people who pay."

"*We're* the people who pay," Amira said. "And we were told the Netherlands. I need to go to the Netherlands."

"What's the difference?" the driver asked.

"So I can get into Germany," Amira said.

"Well now it's Belgium," said the driver.

"Where in Belgium?" Malik asked.

"Ostend," the driver said.

Amira had never heard of Ostend, but it didn't sound like a place she wanted to go. "Will there be a hospital?" she asked. "I have a sick child."

"There'll be a hospital," the driver said. "It's a big place. A city. Not far from the Netherlands."

"How long?" Amira asked.

The driver checked the digital clock above the windscreen. "A few hours . . . Belgium is good for you people. A lot of immigrants."

Malik looked at Amira and shook his head. He cursed at the driver and stormed off. Amira followed him along the aisle. She flopped into her seat. All she wanted to do was get off the coach. To get Rima some attention and go her own way.

One thing that nagged at her: why would they change the destination? What did they care where they ended up? They had their money. Why not dump them by the side of the road in Austria or Germany, the first chance they got?

Her European geography wasn't the best, but she felt sure Belgium was a longer drive than the Netherlands. Another border. And she *knew* it was further from Hungary than Vienna or Munich. Why would the people booking the coach pay for extra fuel and longer hours for the driver?

The questions played on her mind as the coach made its way to Ostend. Something was wrong. *Very* wrong.

Chapter 10

I walk the streets rather than take the bus. I'm twenty pence short and my severance pay for the kitchen job won't hit my bank until the end of the week.

It's an hour's walk home, including a couple of wrong turns. Still finding my way around this place. Half of London looks the same to me. Especially once the shops and bars drop off and you get into the housing estates.

Your money doesn't stretch far down here, either. But it's a good place to get lost in. The best in the country. And since the law froze my assets and accounts, the more lost I get, the better.

The bedsit I'm staying in makes my old flat in Manchester look like the Taj Mahal. It's in a grotty part of the city in a high-rise block. The usual story: gangs fighting each other for turf no one in their right mind would touch.

I walk past 'em now. A handful of young lads. A mix of races. All with one injury or another. A cut face, a black-eye. One kid with his arm in a sling. They block the entrance to the flats, sitting on the steps, dressed in sportswear and jewellery. Rap music blares out of an old school ghetto blaster. I stop in front of 'em.

There's a tense moment. They look at me. I look at them.

They get up and step aside, pulling up their pants as they fall off their arses.

They shuffle into two orderly lines. They nod at me. I nod back.

We had a disagreement when I first moved in. Guns. Knives. Threatening residents. Me included.

I soon sorted that out. A little pro bono fixer work. Just like old times.

They leave the locals alone and I leave them alone. That's the deal. In fact, I've even seen 'em helping struggling mums with their shopping. No doubt they terrorise the surrounding neighbourhoods, but not here.

One of them fist bumps me. I don't know what's wrong with a handshake, but I go with it.

My bedsit is on the second floor. The block of flats overlooks a busy fly-over that passes right by my only window.

After wrestling open the wonky, rusty keyhole, I fiddle with the latch until it locks behind me. From a sunny start to the morning, the day has turned grey. As grey as the overpass that blasts and rattles the paper-thin walls.

The bedsit is dark and uneven. Damp crawls up the corners of the room. The knee-high fridge makes more racket than a nun's vibrator. The toaster sits on the floor next to it. A black scorch mark underneath on a threadbare blue carpet.

There's a sink against one wall. A door to a toilet and bath on the other. A tiny red sofa bed in the middle and a wind chill factor of minus ten blowing in through cracks in the window frame.

As I stand here and look at my life, I realise I haven't got the money to pay the damn rent.

Yep, this is it. The price of going straight.

I sag at the shoulders. Let out a big sigh. Dig a hand in a trouser pocket and call up a number on my decade-old pay-per-go handset.

Randall picks up on the other end.

"Chris?" I say. "I've thought about it."

Chapter 11

Ostend *was* a city. The driver hadn't lied in that respect. And even though night had fallen by the time they arrived, Amira could tell it was a nice place. The streets were clean and quiet. The buildings tall and well maintained: some modern, some historical.

The coach wound its way through the city to a seafront. A long, straight road. A flat expanse of sand and a black ocean in the distance, with tiny lights out to sea.

The coach came to a rest next to a harbour busy with moored yachts. The driver turned off the engine and opened the doors.

That's when the scramble began. Amira's fellow passengers pulled on their coats and grabbed any belongings they had left. They beat a path for the front of the coach. As if the journey to freedom demanded a sprint finish.

Amira waited for the others to clear. Malik too. She peeled Rima out of her seat and carried her along the aisle. She stepped down and outside. Into a windy, chilly night. She smelled the blustery sea air blowing in from the Atlantic.

It was fresher than the Aegean, but more aggressive with it.

No sooner had she felt the tarmac beneath her feet, she saw the others lining up along the side of the coach. There were more men here, like the man in the coat and scarf in Hungary. They were big and well fed under thick black jackets. And blank behind the eyes.

Malik was the first to protest. A man shoved him backwards against the coach, threatening him with a handgun.

The man had wavy dark hair and slugs for eyebrows. He appeared to be in charge, barking instructions for the other two men to round up the others.

Amira looked to the driver as he stepped off the coach. He shrugged and lit a cigarette. She thought about running. She thought too long, soon dragged into line against the side of the coach.

"What's happening?" she asked in English. "We've paid, now let us go."

"Shut up," the leader said.

"But the girl is sick. I need to get her to a hospital."

The man ignored her. They waited in the cold wind. Then on the leader's command, they found themselves herded to the mouth of a wooden jetty.

They stood close together shivering—confused and afraid. Some passengers had belongings packed in rucksacks and small suitcases. Amira only had Rima, clinging to her for warmth.

She saw the gang leader talking to a middle-aged man at the end of the jetty. The owner of a sailboat from what she could make out. The leader seemed to be offering the man something. An envelope. The owner of the boat refused.

The leader tucked the envelope away. He grabbed the owner by his blue jacket and pushed his gun into his ribs.

Amira strained to hear, but the argument was out of earshot.

A few minutes passed. The owner of the boat disappeared beneath deck. The leader waved his men forward.

"Come on," they said, pushing the group along the jetty.

Amira picked up Rima. She shuffled in line—a dozen or more pairs of feet treading the creaking boards. In the dark, she heard the ringing of a bell in the distance and the sound of water lapping against the jetty supports.

As they neared the boat, Amira saw the black sea spanning out in front of her. It filled her with dread.

The two men stopped the passengers alongside the sailboat. They waved them on, one by one with the barrel of a gun.

Amira was last. Her feet locked rigid to the jetty. At the threat of being shot, she willed herself to step forward.

Her legs shook at the feel of a boat deck. Being forced below made it worse. As she wobbled on the top step, Malik reached up and took Rima off her. Amira steadied herself on a cold, steel handrail. She stepped down into a cramped living quarters overcrowded with the other passengers. There was barely room to breathe. Some people had claimed seats on benches that ran either side of the quarters. Others leaned against a square wooden table in the centre of the low-ceilinged room.

As the onboard engine powered up, Amira felt the

vibration through the soles of her feet.

The gang leader stood at the top of the stairs with the boat owner. They argued in English.

"There are too many people," the owner said. "The yacht isn't designed to—"

"Never mind that," the group leader said. "You've got GPS on-board, right?"

"Well, yes, but—"

"Then programme it in. Let's get going."

"This is madness."

"You want to see your family again? You do what I say."

In a few short minutes, the door to the deck closed. A man with a gun parked himself on the steps, blocking any hope of escape. With the last of the fresh air gone and the movement of the boat, the sickness returned to the pit of Amira's stomach. She tried to ignore it. She approached the man on the steps, leaving Rima with Malik.

"Back off," the man said.

"I need a place for the girl to lie down," Amira said, pointing to Rima. "She's sick."

The man looked at Rima. He let out a sigh of inconvenience and got to his feet, as if it had been a long day for him, too. "Follow me," he said, barging his way through the crowd.

Amira took Rima from Malik and followed the man towards the far end of the quarters. He led her to a thin single bunk with a blue sleeping bag. Three passengers sat shoulder to shoulder on the bed. The man barked at them to move. They stood and allowed Amira in. One, a woman around Amira's age, helped her tuck Rima in under the sleeping bag.

Amira thanked her and took a seat with two others on the edge of the bed, a hand stroking Rima's forehead. The young girl's body was burning up: a rasping cough from her mouth.

The man with the gun turned to leave.

"She needs water," Amira said, pulling at his jacket.

He shook her hand off him, as if she was carrying a disease. Without a word, he pushed his way out through the crowd.

He returned moments later with a chilled plastic bottle of mineral water. "Here," he said, handing it over.

He shoved his way back out again. Amira gave Rima a sip and offered the same to her near neighbours.

The ride on the small white yacht was smoother than the dinghy. Yet Amira felt no safer. Particularly when they left the port. She couldn't see, but she could hear the howl of the wind, feel the rolling of the boat over the swell of the North Sea.

The spotlight above her head was dim and yellow. Even though it was fixed into the ceiling, she could swear it was swaying.

So Amira held onto Rima—less for the young girl's reassurance and more for her own. She breathed deep, once again attempting to quell the sickness within her. The other passengers didn't look too enamoured with the rolling, tilting ride either.

And this time, there was a promise of nothing at journey's end. Nothing but uncertainty at the hands of the three men on-board.

Amira felt as if she was caught in a loop. Only with each turn of events, her situation got worse. Here she was, on another treacherous journey full of fear and sickness in the early hours before dawn.

Abdul had lied in Turkey about the size of the boat she'd be taking to Greece. The man in Hungary had conned her out of thousands, only to send her to Ostend. And after all the miles travelled, she found herself further away from Munich than ever.

Being under the thumb of the gangs was no safer than home, under skies of fire and rubble, streets caked in blood and dust. She cursed herself for leaving Aleppo. But what choice did she have? Her neighbours' homes were empty. Her classroom stripped of children. Some spirited away by fleeing parents. Others with candles lit next to photographs, messages and drawings.

Amira closed her eyes and waited out the journey. The nightmares that had punctuated her sleep came at her in waking hours too. A tangle of screaming people sliding off the dinghy. The icy blast of the water. Dead bodies trapped beneath. Rima's grandmother among them. She felt the air escaping out of her lungs. Her arms and legs tiring. The surface shrinking in the distance above. The sunlight petering out. Rima's pale face flashing in front of hers. Oily black eyes. Face half-eaten by fish. White skin flapping off her cheekbones.

Amira gasped awake. The roll of the boat had levelled off. She felt a bump as it docked.

"Everyone off," the men shouted. "One at a time."

Amira roused Rima from her sleep. Rima cried and resisted. Amira pulled her from her bed and carried her across the emptied living quarters. Malik helped her carry Rima up the steps and off the yacht.

The gang leader marched them along another jetty to a deserted harbour wall.

As soon as she set foot on dry land, Amira's stomach settled. She felt the hard tarmac of a road underfoot. Saw the moon in the sky, close to full. A grey cloud drifting across its dazzling white face. It was the only light around, other than distant orange streetlights from the port town.

"Welcome to the UK," the leader said.

"What are we doing here?" Malik asked.

"You wanted to come to Europe," the leader said. "This is Europe . . . Well, for now."

"I paid for the Netherlands," Amira said.

"You'll pay even more if you don't shut up," the leader said, flicking on a torch. "Now empty your pockets. And your bags."

Any protests were soon extinguished as the men roughed up the passengers. They turned out pockets and dumped the contents of bags onto the tarmac.

They took money, passports, papers and jewellery—off wrists, out of ears and from around necks.

One of the men held open a red polyester bag with a white drawstring. They filled it with cash and valuables.

The gang leader seized Amira's arm. He padded her down. "You're hiding something . . ." His hand lingered around the waist of her trousers. Without warning, he ripped the top button open. Forced a cold, rough hand down the front.

Amira screamed. Malik attempted to intervene. The butt of a gun struck him across the forehead.

The leader felt around Amira's knickers, the tops of her thighs. For a moment, she thought he had missed the money bag. But no, his hand stopped. He tore the bag from its stitching.

He shone the torch over the bag, revealing her passport and a thin wad of Euro notes. It was all that remained of Amira's worldly possessions, save for the clothes on her back.

"Well what have we here?" he said. "Sneaky fucking Arabs."

"What about the kid?" one of his colleagues asked, approaching Rima. "She might be hiding something too."

The man unzipped Rima's coat and shone his torch along the insides. He moved to pad her down.

"Don't touch her!" Amira yelled, fighting to stop him.

The gang leader pulled his man back by the sleeve. "Leave it," he said. "We haven't got time."

"What are we supposed to do?" Malik said. "We've no money, food, passports."

The gang leader looked into the middle distance, to where a twin beam of headlights approached along a coast road. "Don't worry," he said. "Your transport is here."

Chapter 12

Ramsgate, Kent. The south coast of England. It's early when I step off the train. Way too early. The sun hasn't been up long as I exit the tinpot station.

Ramsgate is your typical seaside town. Cottages, bed and breakfasts, small shops and cafés. It's still off-season, so tourists are few.

I set off. A small plastic bag with a rope string on my back, with a bottle of water and a couple of CDs inside. It's only when you get out here, you remember what fresh air tastes and smells like. I hear the cry of gulls. Suck in the sea breeze.

Nothing like it.

If only there was a chippy open. Seaside food always tastes better.

I stride along tiny, quaint streets. I follow a set of directions handed to me by Randall at St Pancras. They're scribbled in black ballpoint on the back of a crumpled e-ticket print-off. They tell me to head towards the harbour.

Through the gaps between cottages, I see the hazy grey

line of the sea against the horizon. I walk towards it and find the promenade. The harbour wall is high. It wraps around a gathering of moored yachts, with a pair of ferries docked further out.

Further down the road is the start of a long stretch of honey-coloured sand. There's a red and white helter-skelter and a large hotel on the seafront. A few people jogging and walking dogs, but no other action besides.

The sea is calm and so is the breeze coming in off the channel. I keep walking. The promenade drops off and along with it, the main body of the town.

I find myself heading out into the sticks, wondering if I've read the directions wrong. Randall always had terrible handwriting.

I walk for another ten minutes along a coastal road. Then I see it, there in the distance. The white cab of a truck facing me. Parked in a lay-by at the side of the road. I check the plate against the reg number written under the directions.

That's the one. A six-wheeler with a fixed trailer. Harder to drive than an articulated wagon, but straightforward enough.

Christ, they must have brought over a lot of fake merchandise. Who knows where it's come from and which designer brands they've ripped off. And who cares? I get my arse back to London for noon and I get five-hundred quid in my back pocket.

I walk around the truck, kicking the tyres. The trailer's unmarked and the rear doors padlocked, but the driver door is open. I climb inside the cab. It's right-hand drive. I find a folded map between the dash and windscreen. There's an air freshener hanging from the rear view mirror: bright orange in the shape of the letter *M*.

It smells of citrus.

It's been a long time since I've driven anything like this. I find the keys in the passenger visor, exactly where Randall said they'd be. I catch them and turn the diesel engine over. The truck rumbles and the cabin shakes. I let the engine warm as I take out my bottle of water and wedge it in the cup holder in a central console. I adjust the mirrors, belt up and turn up the radio: early morning sports chatter. I put the truck into gear and away we go.

The roads are dead. The muscle memory still there from the old days. I reminisce about when I used to hijack armed lorries and transporter trucks with a crew.

We'd drive 'em away, leaving the guards gagged and bound by the side of the road.

Great days. Simpler days.

I swing the truck over a couple of roundabouts and head out of Ramsgate.

Chapter 13

I crank up the stereo. "Sweet Caroline" by Neil Diamond. Not my personal favourite, but still a great tune. I sing my lungs out as the truck chugs along at fifty.

I'm trying to keep the speed reasonable so I don't draw attention from any arsehole traffic cops. They have a nasty habit of hiding in cars behind bushes with their speed guns.

The last thing I need is them asking me who I am, or what I'm carrying.

But I need to make time, too.

As I slow down for a queue at a roundabout, I grab the map off the dash and open it out against the steering wheel. I run a finger along the A-roads to London, seeing if there's a faster way back to the city. If I don't get there on time, I don't get paid. That was the deal, Randall said. And a cushy number like this once a week . . . I'll soon be out of that bedsit.

So yeah, it's not legal what I'm doing. But the only bloke I'm hurting is Giorgio Armani. Even Cassie wouldn't have a problem with that.

***

I find myself a quicker route. It'll save me twenty minutes. Which means I can afford to stop the truck in a lay-by. I climb out to take a piss. Stretch my legs. An hour and twenty still to drive. It's not even nine-thirty yet. Plenty of time. I wander into the long grass by the side of the road. I piss in the field, looking out across an open stretch of wild grass ruffling in the wind.

As I'm shaking the old chap off, I think I hear something behind me. I zip up and turn to face the truck.

Thought I heard a knocking sound.

I listen hard. With cars flying past at sixty and seventy, it's not easy. I bend over and look underneath the truck. I move over to the cab. The engine's still running. Could it be coming from there?

Don't tell me the bloody thing's got a problem.

I listen some more.

Nah, just hearing things. Must be the lack of sleep. That wafer-thin sofa bed is killing me. I walk around the front of the cab and climb back into the driver's seat, pull on my belt, release the brakes and indicate. I wait for a clear stretch of road and ease back onto the dual carriageway.

I bring the truck up to a steady fifty and eject the CD in the stereo. One eye on the road, the other on my bag, as I rummage inside for the other disc.

Then I hear it again. That bumping, banging sound. Kind of muffled. Not from the engine. Almost like it's behind my seat, from inside the trailer. I wonder if it's a loose box or pallet, knocking against the inside trailer wall.

Yeah, probably a loose pallet.

I ignore it for a while. Turn up the next song.

But it bugs the shit out of me.

The sound isn't random enough. It's in a pattern. One minute it's quick, the next it's slow. Always in a sequence, like someone trying different knocks on a door.

I decide to pull over at the next lay-by. Five minutes down the road, I find something even better. An empty stretch of concrete signposted as a sleepover for truck drivers.

I pull off the road and spin the wagon around so it's facing the carriageway.

I turn off the engine and reach across the cabin. Pop the glove box and rummage inside. Nothing but old dockets and manifests.

Damn, I was hoping to find a key for that padlock.

I jump down out of the truck and walk around to the back of the trailer. I take out the burner phone Randall gave me with his number pre-programmed in. Something heavy bumps against the inside of the trailer doors. I dial Randall's number. He answers as if I woke him up. A heavy night on the booze and blackjack tables, knowing him.

"Uh, hello?"

"Chris?"

"Breaker?"

"Are you sure it's fake merch in the back of this truck?"

"What do you mean?"

"I mean, I'm not transporting a bloody gorilla or crocodile or something."

"Huh?"

"Fake handbags don't tend to bang on trailer doors, Chris."

"Listen, Charlie. Where are you?"

"Not sure. A truck stop somewhere. I can find out."

"Never mind," he says. "We'll have you on GPS. Hold on a second."

I hear Randall in the background. He tells a girlfriend to leave the room. He seems to be having a conversation with someone else on another phone.

I don't hear what he says, but he comes back on the line. "Okay, someone's gonna come and take a look. They're not too far from you."

"*Someone?* Like who?"

"Someone with a key. They'll be thirty minutes, tops."

"What about the delivery?" I ask, checking my watch. "I'm gonna be late."

"Don't worry about that," Randall says. "I'll see you get paid. Just sit tight."

"Alright, but why don't I take a look now? It's padlocked, but I can open it up easy."

"Charlie, I'm just the middleman. It's not my truck. Sit tight, yeah?"

"Alright then," I say.

Randall hangs up on me. I slip the burner inside a trouser pocket. More bumps from behind the trailer door. I stretch my legs out. Check my watch. Lean against the side of the truck. Climb back inside the cabin.

Sod it.

I reach behind the seats. Open the lid on a black toolbox and pull out a tyre iron.

I jump down again and return to the rear of the trailer. I wedge the tyre iron in the padlock and force it to pop out. I slide the bolts open on the trailer doors.

I know Randall said not to. But what's the worst that could be in there, right?

Unless they *have* got a wild animal in there. A tiger. A bear. You never know with eBay.

I open the doors real slow. The left one, then the right.

Oh, it's not a tiger or a bear.

It's something far, far worse.

Chapter 14

The smell hits me first. Stale air and bodies. Out of the gloom blink a dozen pairs of eyes. I fold both doors all the way open to let in the light. I look up and see 'em sitting either side of the trailer floor. Shivering and huddling over. There's a tiny body lying prone in the centre of the dusty wood panel floor. It's a child under a coat.

A young woman kneels next to the young kid. She's pretty and slim. Black hair tied into a loose ponytail. She looks Arabic to me. Most of 'em do, other than a few who look African.

They stare at me with tired eyes and drawn faces, breathing in the air like they've been suffocating.

Did they stow away on the truck? No, there'd be boxes and pallets in the back too. They're the only cargo I'm carrying.

"Anyone speak English?" I ask.

The young woman raises a hand. "Is this the UK?"

"Looks like it," I say. "Where have you come from?"

"Syria," she says. "And Libya, Afghanistan, Somalia."

"No, I mean, how did you get here?"

"We took a boat, from Ostend," a man says, from somewhere in the gloom.

"Where?"

"A port in Belgium," the young woman says.

"You crossed the channel?"

"Yes, in a small yacht, overnight. They paid out of our money."

"Who's *they*?"

"I don't know," she says, gesturing to the young kid. "Listen, the child is sick. And we can't breathe in here."

"I'm not surprised," I say, "there's no ventilation."

Another guy from the back says something. He's irate.

The woman translates. "He wants to know if we can get out now."

"No," I say. The last thing I want is a bunch of migrants spilling out of my truck. You don't know who's watching. Police, passing motorists . . . "Stay in here," I say.

"You can't leave us by the side of the road," the woman says.

"It won't be long," I say, holding out both hands. "Help is coming. I'll leave the doors open."

The woman continues to whinge. "The child, she needs help now."

"Is she yours?" I ask.

She shakes her head. "She doesn't have parents."

"Well where the hell are they?"

A woman sitting to the left of me speaks. She's in her forties and wrapped in a purple headscarf. She makes a movement with her hand like a missile landing. No translation needed.

I check my watch and glance around the side of the truck, getting anxious. *Where are these pricks?*

I take out my phone and walk away from the truck, keeping an eye on the people inside. I call Randall.

"Breaker?"

"Did you know?" I ask.

"Know what?"

"What the cargo was."

"No, I told you . . . Why, what did you do?"

"Opened it up, didn't I?"

"Why the fuck did you do that?"

"Never mind why I did it, it's a good job I did."

Randall goes quiet on me.

"Well, are you gonna ask me or what?"

"Listen, whatever it is, Charlie, I don't wanna know."

"Maybe you can guess instead," I say. "Your fake merch has come all the way from Syria. And I bet not one of them is called Giorgio Armani."

"You're not saying what I think you're saying—"

"You know exactly what I'm saying, Chris. What do I do with 'em?"

I can hear the cogs turning in Randall's head from here. "Look, the plan's the same. Sit tight until help arrives. They'll sort you out."

"Is that it?"

"What do you want me to say, Charlie? We've both been fed the same bullshit."

I realise it's as much of a shock for Randall as it is for me, so I cool my own jets. "Okay fine, I'll call you when I know something."

I end the conversation and return to the trailer.

The woman who speaks English is straight back on my case. "What about the girl?" she asks. "She needs a doctor."

"What's wrong with her?" I ask, stepping up into the trailer.

"I don't know," she says. "It looks serious."

It's gloomy inside the trailer, but as daylight spills in, I see the young girl's face. Pale and sweating cold.

I notice tiny salt crystals in her hair. "She fall in the Channel or something?"

"No, near Greece. A big wave hit us," the woman says. "The boat tipped over."

I whip off my bomber jacket. "Well why didn't you say so?" I fold up the jacket and raise the girl's head. Her hair is stiff and straggled. "I reckon she's got hypothermia."

"What's that?" she asks.

"It's urgent, that's what it is."

"I told you," she says.

As we're talking, I hear tyres over concrete. The double pip of a car horn. "Give her this as well," I say, tugging at the woman's red wool jumper. "Keep her as warm as you can."

The woman nods and removes her jumper. Underneath, she wears a salmon pink shirt with sleeves rolled up to the elbows. Plus a pair of mud-stained khaki trousers and battered silver trainers.

I turn and jump down from the trailer. The car is a metallic-blue Vauxhall saloon. It drives past the truck to my right. Parks up twenty feet away, the engine running. Like they're getting a look at me first.

After a long minute, driver and passenger climb out and I get a good look at them.

The pair of 'em are a front page special—bad news. War. Famine. Earthquakes. That kind of bad news. They're a couple of heavy-treading bruisers in black jeans and leather coats. One, a bald white guy with a gold chain and no chin. The other, a dark-skinned bloke with a low-rising mohawk. Not the people you send to have a conversation.

I back off a few feet. Put a hand on the left hand door. I close it.

My human cargo starts to protest. Especially when I swing the other door shut.

"It's only for a minute," I say to the young woman.

As the two goons get close, I can tell they're carrying. Not exactly surprising, but not reassuring either. They stop short of me around the rear of the trailer. Shoulder to shoulder, like bouncers minding a door.

"So what's the situation?" I ask.

"You come with us," says the white guy in a Baltic accent.

"What about the truck?"

"Never mind about the truck," the darker one says in a cockney voice.

"There's a sick girl in there."

"So?" the white guy says.

"So she needs help, bowling ball."

They look at me with blank expressions.

"They've got no ventilation," I say.

The cockney shrugs.

"Don't you want me to drive it?" I ask. "I can at least finish the job."

"Nah it's alright, leave it," the cockney says.

"Listen mate," I say, "you can't just leave 'em here."

"They already pay," the foreign guy says.

The cockney nods towards the car. "Come on."

I look at the truck. At the two men. "What if I say no?"

"We're not asking," says the cockney.

The foreign one pulls the left lapel of his jacket open. Shows me a piece holstered against his ribs.

"Alright, after you," I say. "I still get paid though, right?"

"You'll get what's due," the cockney says, leading the way.

Of course they're not gonna pay me. They're gonna drive me somewhere quiet and shoot me in the skull. They'll leave the truck and move on. It's not like anyone's gonna miss me, or a trailer full of dead migrants.

We reach the car. Baldy opens a door for me. I get in the back, behind the driver seat. He squeezes his frame behind the wheel and starts the engine. The cockney gets in across from me on the backseat.

Baldy puts the car in reverse.

The cockney sneers at me. "Where's that accent from?"

"Manchester."

He laughs to himself. "Northern twat."

See, this is the problem with the youth of today. They're overconfident.

They don't know what they don't know.

And they don't *know* that they don't know it.

For starters, they've already shown me where they holster their weapons. *And* they let me pick my own spot on the backseat.

Oh dear, oh dear.

Chapter 15

As Baldy backs up the car, I make my move.

I double over and yank a lever to the bottom right of the seat in front.

I pull the seat all the way back so the driver's almost lying down. I reach around front and beat his hand to the gun in his jacket.

As the cockney goes for his own weapon, I twist the holster and pull the trigger.

A bullet punches a hole through the driver's leather jacket. It hits the cockney in the left shoulder. He rocks back in his seat, but still goes for his gun. I swing the point of my left hand into his throat.

Baldy wrestles me for the pistol. It drops to the floor. I yank his seatbelt away from the door pillar and wrap it fast around his throat.

The cockney finally pulls out his weapon. I smack it out of his hand and it gets lost in the footwell.

The car keeps reversing, heading towards the trees and bushes behind the truck stop.

I pull the belt tighter to speed up the choke on the driver. I feel a cracking pain in my left cheek. The cockney slamming a ring-fingered fist in my face. I duck away from the next punch and twist in my seat with my legs in the air.

I drive my right boot into the cockney's face. I press my left boot against his windpipe and force his head back against the rear passenger window.

I put the other boot against his forehead. I push as hard as I can. He tries to force my legs off, but I've got 'em locked at the knee.

As I pull down hard on the seatbelt with my right hand, I hear Baldy choke out. I draw back my right boot and drive it hard into the cockney's jaw.

There's a deep crack. His neck breaking as his head twists in a way it wasn't designed to.

I let go of the belt and reach under the driver's seat.

I snatch Baldy's gun from the holster and push the seat forward.

I jack open the passenger door and roll out backwards onto the concrete. I tumble a couple of times as the car drifts into the bushes. It rolls right in there, disappearing from sight.

Getting to my feet, I dust myself down. I check the chamber of the gun. It's empty, but the clip is almost full.

I turn my attention to the truck. I jog over and open the trailer doors. The people in the back are still cowering, shoved up away from the sound of gunfire.

The young woman kneels next to the girl, stroking her hair.

I hop up inside the trailer. "You," I say to her, "get out."

She looks at the weapon in my hand. Wide-eyed and worried.

I tuck the gun away in the back of my jeans. "Here," I say, scooping up the sick girl. "It's warmer in the front. Follow me."

I jump down with the girl. Nothing but a quaking bundle in my arms. Her eyes half-closed in pain. I walk around to the passenger side and open the door. I climb in with the girl and lay her down on a small cot behind the seats.

There's a thin white mattress and a navy blanket on top, plus a small pillow perfect for the girl's head.

The young woman climbs in the cab behind me. She tucks the girl in as I back my way out and return to the trailer. I jump up and take out the gun.

The people in the trailer shrink away in fear.

"Hands over ears," I say, demonstrating the action.

They clap their hands against the sides of their heads. I angle the barrel towards the ceiling. I let off three rounds into the roof of the trailer. Three evenly-spaced holes let in a supply of fresh air and daylight. Better in the roof than the side of the truck. No one will see the bullet holes.

"Sit tight," I say. "Won't be long now."

They look at me like I'm talking gibberish. I shrug and jump out of the trailer. I swing the doors shut and fasten them up. Just in time, too. Another truck pulls over into the stop. A big articulated lorry with a blue cab and a long orange trailer. The driver honks his horn as he pulls past me.

I give him a wave and climb behind the wheel. The little girl is tucked in tight. The young woman in the passenger seat.

"How's she doing?" I ask.

"I don't think she has long," the woman says.

I grab the map off the dash and run a finger over the roads. I look for the nearest major town.

Guildford.

I tap the point on the map. "Here, we'll find a hospital."

I slide the map on the dash and start the engine. I pull the truck out of the stop and we hit the road.

Chapter 16

I overtake a silver people carrier driving at the speed of cold sludge. The truck's giving me no more than seventy, but at least we're making time as we roll downhill. The woman returns to her seat after tending to the girl.

"How's the kid?" I ask.

"She's stopped shivering."

"That's a good sign, right?"

"I don't think so," the woman says. "How long?"

"Depends on traffic. Maybe twenty minutes. Then we've got to find the hospital." I look across at the woman. Dark circles frame her round brown eyes, as if she hasn't slept in days. "What's your name?"

"Amira." she says.

"I'm Charlie," I say, turning the wheel to overtake a red Nissan Micra.

"What happened earlier?" Amira asks.

"Two of your smugglers came for me. I had to sort 'em out."

"You're not one of them?" she asks.

"I'm just a guy driving a truck. Didn't realise it was full of migrants. What have you come over for, jobs? 'Cause there ain't many."

"We're not here because of work. Most of us are professionals. Scientists, Engineers . . . I'm a teacher."

"Then why are you in the back of a bloody truck?"

"It's not safe at home. And we heard we'd be welcome in Europe."

I burst out laughing. "Yeah, about as welcome as a fart in a lift."

Amira looks confused.

"It means asylum seekers aren't too popular over here," I say.

"Does that include you?" she asks.

"Me? I couldn't give a toss, love."

"A toss?"

"It means . . . Er, what I mean is, I'm like Switzerland." She looks at me funny again. I'm confusing her even more. "I'm neutral. I don't care one way or the other. But then again, I've been cash-in-hand most of my life."

"You mean truck drivers don't pay tax?"

"I didn't say I was a truck driver."

"Then what's your profession?" Amira asks me.

"At the moment? Unemployed waiter."

"Oh," she says.

"Yeah, at my age." I say, steering the truck back to the inside lane. "How much did you pay those smugglers?"

"What does it matter?" Amira says. "They stole everything from us. Money. Passports. Everything."

I whistle. *"Jesus."* I slow the truck for an upcoming roundabout. "You shouldn't have gone near those guys. I hear they're brutal."

"It was the only way," Amira says, steadying herself with a hand on the dash.

I swing the truck around the roundabout and take the third exit. As I'm accelerating away, I glance over my shoulder at the young girl. She coughs and whimpers. Amira flies out of her seat to comfort her. With a hand on her forehead, she speaks soft words to her in her own language.

I get us up to speed again and see a sign for Guildford. Next junction and we're there. I wonder if I should call Randall. Maybe I can sort this lot out in the back after we drop the young girl off at the hospital . . . *If* she makes it.

I reach inside my jeans pocket for the burner phone. I rest it against the wheel and toggle through the tiny blue screen for Randall's number.

Out of the corner of my eye, I see a tall white cab pull alongside, detached from its trailer. The driver's a bulldog in blue overalls. He turns his wheel hard to the left.

What the bloody hell?

The cab shunts into us. The phone spills from my hand, lost in the footwell as we take the hit. We veer off to the left. I straighten us out, back onto the road. The cab comes again. Hits us even harder. Metal crunching against metal. I steer it straight again.

Amira's in a panic. *"What's going on?"*

"Just a wild guess, but I'd say your smugglers want their merch back. Hold on."

As the bulldog in that cab turns his wheel again, I turn mine to the left, swerving another attack. Then I turn right, giving him a taste of his own medicine. But his cab is bigger than this one. Made of sterner stuff too. And there's another problem.

We take a hit from behind. A heavy one.

I lurch forward in my seat. Amira sprawls over the dash. The girl rolls halfway out of bed.

As Amira gathers herself and sees to the girl, I check my mirrors. I see another unmarked white cab easing back into view, lining up for another go.

At the speed we're travelling, there's little danger of us catching any of the cars up ahead. But the problem isn't the cars. It's things like other trucks and coaches on the road. I see the cab come at us again, faster than we are without its trailer.

We take another shunt. Amira holds on to the bed and the girl.

At almost the same time, the cab alongside swings into us. The steering wheel judders under both impacts.

They force us left. The hard shoulder not enough to save us from a steel barrier and a sheer drop over a bridge.

I think fast and slam on the brakes. The tyres scream as they fight the speed of the cab behind. But we slow enough for his mate on the right to slide off us and shoot past. I steer back onto the carriageway. Saved for the time being, but I've gotta do something. Gotta think.

"Here, take the wheel,".

"What?" Amira says. "I can't."

"Take the wheel or we all die," I say, opening the driver door.

"I don't know how," she yells.

"Sure you do. Just keep your foot on the pedal and hold it steady."

"What about you?" she asks.

"Forget about me. If you can take the next exit, take it."

I don't give her much choice. I'm already halfway out of the door with one hand on the wheel and a toe on the accelerator. Amira slides into the driver's seat behind me. Her head an eyebrow above the wheel and legs stretching to reach the pedals. I hang half out of the door. Eyes watering. Body buffeted by the wind.

I wait for the cab in front to pull to the right. The brake lights go on. It's dropping back for another round.

When he's a few feet away, I make the jump. I land on the rear tractor axle behind the cab. As the truck lines up with mine, I climb around the driver side.

Holding onto a grab handle, I fling the door open and reach inside. The bulldog behind the wheel pulls a shotgun on me. I slam the door shut on his hand. The gun falls away and the guy screams in pain. I hit him twice in the face. The cab swerves left into Amira. I see her through the passenger window. She wrestles with the steering, scared out of her mind. I pull the wheel of the cab to the right, giving her a chance to correct. The bulldog catches me with a heavy punch to the ribs. He fights me for control. I plant an elbow hard between his eyes and he goes loose. I grab him by the overalls and throw him out of the cab.

Right. Now let's sort this other dickhead out.

I hit the brakes and drop back alongside the cab behind our truck. As the driver brings it in for another bump from behind, I steer left and knock him off his path. He comes back at me. We jostle left and right, trading blows. It takes the heat off Amira, but I'm soon ducking low in my seat. Another shotgun and a man who isn't shy on using it.

I stay down low, windows and windscreen full of bullet holes. I see another bridge crossing coming up.

It's a chance.

I wait for the right moment. I pull a hard left with everything I've got. As the remaining driver lets off another round, I slam my cab into his, pushing him left and sticking with it.

I see the look of panic on his face. He drops the gun and fights to correct. I straighten up in the nick of time. But it's too late for the other driver. His cab smashes through a steel barrier. It flies off the edge of the bridge, plunging towards the river below.

I give the cab the full beans, cranking through the gears and catching up to Amira. The dual carriageway drops to a single lane as we near the exit, with cars and trucks coming the other way. I'm forced onto the inside, the hard shoulder. I come up alongside Amira. This is gonna be tricky.

Trickier still, thanks to a small mountain of grit and dirt piled up by the roadside.

I've got five-hundred metres before I hit the stuff.

I open my door and switch my left foot to the accelerator. My right foot on the doorsill, left hand on the wheel and the other reaching out for a hold of the truck.

Dirt Mountain is coming up fast. The exit right after it. The ground rushes beneath my feet. I jump at the last second. I catch hold of the door handle but my feet slip off.

I hold on for dear life. The cab ploughs into the dirt. The stuff explodes into the air: soil, grit and sand raining all over me as the soles of my boots clip the tarmac. I haul myself up and open the door. I slide inside the truck and slam the door shut.

Amira can't wait to hand over control. As we switch places, I notice the Guildford exit about to pass us by. I swing left into the slip road, cutting up a car towing a caravan. The exit ramp is steep and slows us in time to join a big, busy roundabout. I follow the road to Guildford and see signs for a hospital.

The truck is bruised and battered.

Amira's shaken up.

I'm bloody knackered. Grit in my mouth and sand in my eye. I crank up the fan heaters and step on the accelerator.

Chapter 17

By some kind of miracle, the police have yet to catch up with us. Something tells me they won't be far behind after that three-way truck battle.

I swing the lorry into the emergency drop-off area of the Royal Surrey County Hospital.

I scoop up the girl, blanket and all. I make for Accident & Emergency. Amira jumps out behind me. She wants to stay with her.

"No," I say. "Stay with the truck. I'll dump her and run."

"Someone needs to be with her. I made a promise—"

"The police will get hold of you."

"I don't care," she says.

"Well do you care about your friends in the back? 'Cause if that truck gets towed, they're either dead or deported."

Amira throws her arms up in the air. "Okay," she says, staying with the truck.

I run inside with the girl, shouting my lungs off. An ageing, dreadlocked nurse comes running. She asks what's wrong with the girl.

"Hypothermia," I say. "She fell in the sea."

"How long ago?" the nurse asks, feeling the girl's pulse.

"I dunno," I say. "But she's on death's door."

The nurse calls over a junior doctor. A young Indian guy with floppy black hair. I hand over the girl.

"Will she be okay?" I shout as they rush off with her.

"Stay here," the nurse yells back, as they disappear around a corner.

I look around me. An A&E waiting room full of sick and miserable people. I flash a woman on reception an innocent smile and stride off.

I come out of the automatic doors as an ambulance pulls in, beeping at our truck. I wave a hand in apology and hop inside the cab. I swing the truck out of the carpark and find a quiet street. It's lined by a factory wall on one side and a series of shuttered lockups on the other.

"I'll check on the others," Amira says, climbing out of the passenger door.

"Be discreet," I say. "Don't let them get out."

I reach into the footwell and run my hand along the carpet. I retrieve the burner and see three missed calls from Randall.

I call him up.

"Charlie, what the fuck's going on? You were supposed to call me."

"Yeah, well I was a little pre-occupied," I say, stepping down, from the cab. I walk around the back of the trailer, keeping an eye out both ways. "The important thing is I've got a wagon full of refugees and nowhere to put 'em."

"Where are you?" Randall asks.

"Guildford. Near the hospital. Though I don't fancy hanging around for too long."

I cast an eye over the people in the trailer. They look even more afraid than before. Not surprised after the battering we took on the way in here.

"Listen," Randall says. "I reckon I've got a solution that'll work for all parties. You got a paper and pen?"

"Hang on," I say jogging back to the cab. I reach inside a compartment in the door and dig out a chewed blue biro. I retrieve the map. Randall talks me through the directions to a suggested meeting place. I draw a line from our current location to the nearest junction on the map. "Right," I say. "See you in an hour." I come off the phone. "Everyone okay?" I ask Amira.

"Yes, but they need water," she says, climbing into the cab.

I roll the truck a few hundred yards down the road, stopping outside a glass office building. I notice an unmanned reception desk on the ground floor. "Wait here," I say.

I enter the building through a revolving door. I take a lift up to the first floor. Security is light here. The smell of fresh paint on the walls. They're still getting themselves sorted.

I walk straight in through a spacious kitchen, into an open plan office.

The key here is confidence. A nonchalant boredom, as if you do this all day, every day.

I'm looking for a water cooler.

Oh, even easier.

There's one right next to me as I enter the office. I don't even have to disconnect the barrel: there's a spare one sitting next to the base of the unit.

I hoist it up over a shoulder and carry it out. I grab two supermarket bags from the staff kitchen on my way out. They're full of crisps, sandwiches and chocolate bars. I take the stairs rather than the lift and ghost out of reception. I open a trailer door and slide the water barrel inside.

They can figure the rest out for themselves. I take a few things from the bags before sliding them in.

The first chance I get, I stop at a petrol station and fill up the truck. I buy two bottles of water for me and Amira. I find my way back to the A-roads and onto another dual carriageway out of Guildford.

Amira downs half a litre bottle of water, spilling some on the neck of her shirt. She demolishes a sandwich and a Snickers.

I check in my mirrors, expecting blue flashing lights. The cops haven't caught up with us yet, but it's only a matter of time.

Gotta get us off these roads.

I consult the map again. A few more miles and I'll be rid of this whole bloody nightmare.

Chapter 18

The meeting place is on the outskirts of London. It's a stalled building project on a patch of deserted land. Black wooden hoardings with CGI impressions of a factory. The name of the developer, *Taylor Williams*, is written in fancy gold type on the boards.

And little white signs dotted around saying: *Property of VX Holdings. Trespassers Will Be Prosecuted.*

I get out of the truck and find the chain around the gates isn't locked. I guess they'll just have to prosecute me, 'cause I open the gates and steer the truck onto the site. The ground is a mix of soil, stone and building sand. The truck wheels splash through big, horrible puddles of milky-brown water. I follow a track made by digger wheels. We bump and trundle past square pits dug deep in the ground. Some with giant foundation pins driven in. Some filled in with cement. Others left empty.

It looks like one of those places you see where the money ran out and they abandoned the project.

Halfway across the site, I spot a grey Portakabin at the

far end. I park up in front of it. This is where Randall said to meet, but there's no sign of him yet. I turn off the engine. Amira looks at me like: *is this it?*

"Don't worry," I say. "We won't be here long."

We climb out of the truck. I walk around back and open up the trailer. The water in the barrel is halfway gone and the two shopping bags are full of empty food wrappers.

One of the men, his eyes sunken and his body lean, has his hands over his crotch. He speaks English too. "I need to go."

"Okay pal," I say. "Hold on a second."

I check around the rear of the Portakabin. There's a freestanding blue Portaloo. I open the door. The toilet bowl is empty, lined up over a hole in the ground. It isn't pretty, but it'll do.

I take a piss myself, then return and point the guy in the direction of the loo. He hops out of the truck, squinting in the grey London skies. The others follow suit. They form an orderly, snaking queue to the Portaloo.

I text Randall and let him know we've arrived.

It's chilly out here. Nothing standing in the way of the wind. So I take a look at the Portakabin door.

It's locked.

I put my foot through it.

Not anymore.

I turn on the heaters in the cabin and invite my relieved human cargo inside. One by one, they return, filling up the cabin, crowding around the heaters to get warm. Not used to our tropical spring climate.

Crammed inside the Portakabin, we wait for Randall to arrive. Whatever plan he's come up with, I know it'll be a good one. He's not an enforcer like I used to be: the scary character who breaks your door in and puts a gun in your mouth. No, he has a way of thinking around problems. The last time we worked together, there was a big falling out between the north and south. All-out war for a contract with a big Dutch supplier. Pills, weed, coke, stuff like that.

Anyway, they fought for sole control for two years. Revenge attacks every other week. Neither side backing down. After they got tired of spilling blood, both bosses saw sense and sent in their two best fixers.

We met in the middle. A service station near Birmingham. We thrashed it out over a Big Mac meal. Randall came up with a plan to pool resources and double the size of the operation. They split it fifty-fifty, which meant neither side's balance sheet took a hit. In the end, they tripled their profits across the board: drugs, hookers, stolen goods, the whole lot. And we all lived happily ever after.

Well, for a while at least.

Point is, it opened my eyes to a new way of doing things. I started to think around problems for a change. Hurt fewer people. Get better results. Up my rates in the process.

The Double Dutch Plan went so well, the two sides paired me and Randall as a team. We became good mates after that, until Randall got sent down. He got done for glassing a guy in a pub of all things. Though in defence of Randall, the guy was shagging his now ex-missus.

After a thirty-minute wait, I hear engines approaching

the cabin. I step outside and walk around the front of the lorry. I see two grey Volkswagen people carriers approaching, along with a silver van and a dark-blue Land Rover bringing up the rear. They park up twenty feet away. Randall gets out of the Land Rover. A guy out of the van. Two more out of those VWs.

They all look as if they can handle themselves.

Randall shakes his head as he approaches. "Sorry mate, if I'd have known, I never would have put you forward."

He extends a hand. I shake it. "Don't worry pal," I say. "So long as you've got a fix."

Randall breaks into a smile. "That I have," he says, glancing inside the empty trailer. "Where are they hiding?"

I nod towards the Portakabin. "Keeping warm. Poor bastards."

"Then let's get 'em sorted," Randall says, signalling the drivers of the people carriers.

The two men open the sliding doors to the VWs. I lead Randall into the Portakabin.

I speak to the room. "Time to go."

There's chatter among the refugees.

"First you tell us where we are going," Amira says. "We still haven't been told."

Randall addresses the room. Amira translates for a few who speak her language.

"We've got a couple of empty houses not far from here," Randall says. "We'll take you straight there. You can get a warm bed, a nice shower. You can wash your clothes and we'll get you something to eat."

"What about passports?" Amira asks. "They were taken."

"We'll need a few days to look into it. In the meantime, there'll be work for anyone who wants it. Pay at the end of the day, in cash."

Amira translates. A few of the refugees nod and smile. It seems to convince the others.

"Okay folks," Randall says. "Follow me."

The group trail us out to the people carriers. A couple of the refugees acknowledge me. A nod. A handshake. A look in the eye.

Amira is the last one to climb in. She puts a hand on my arm. "Are you sure about these men?" she asks.

"Chris is a mate of mine," I say. "I can vouch for him."

I can see she's still not convinced, so I pull her in close for a hug. I take out the burner Chris gave me. I'm discreet about it, speeding through the contacts and finding the number for the phone. I commit it to memory using a technique I learned years ago. Handy when you need to remember alarm and safe codes. I slip the burner in Amira's trouser pocket, unseen to anyone else. "Here," I say. "I'll call and check on you."

I let her go. She nods and climbs inside the second of the VWs. I slide the passenger door shut. I wait for the two people carriers to take off. But I realise the drivers are missing.

I see Amira's eyes widen. She shouts my name, muffled by the glass. She bangs on the window and pulls at the door handle.

I turn around too late. Catch the end of something hard

and heavy on my nose. Take a whack in the ribs and a stinging smack behind my right leg. I drop to one knee, trying to get my bearings.

But that was the appetiser. Now the main course. I'm forced to the ground. I lie on the floor, trying to cover up while the three drivers beat the shit out of me. Steel baseball bats with my blood all over 'em.

I see the Land Rover boot wide open. I wasn't paying attention. While my back was turned, they were tooling up good and proper. I fight to get to my feet. The drivers kick me while I'm down. A steel toe boot in the side. Another in the head.

I look up, hanging on to consciousness. The drivers stand over me.

Randall too, smoking a cig. "Sorry Breaker, but I told you not to open those doors."

He knew. He knew all along, the scheming little fucker.

"You piece of fucking shit," I say . . . I think I say. Whether the words come out, I don't know.

"If there was any other way mate . . ." Randall says. "But the people I work for now . . . They've given the order."

Work for? Order? He's supposed to be the middleman. Independent. Guess he must have sold out. Gone corporate.

I squirm on the floor, desperate. Feet kicking out for traction. Handfuls of dirt, drained of energy. My vision blurred. My hearing woolly. The drivers all look the same: burly and mean.

I realise I'm seeing three of the same guy. I see a flash of baseball bat swinging towards my head.

Nothing but sounds now. Voices.

"You want me to pop one in him?" one of the drivers asks.

"No," Randall says. "The sound'll travel for miles around here. Besides, he's only got a few minutes left in him . . . Me and Terry'll take the foreigners to the compound. You two bury him with the other one, then get rid of the truck."

I hear 'em say "*yes boss*".

Then no sounds at all.

I feel like I'm rolling, falling.

Falling into a deep, dark hole.

Chapter 19

I open my eyes. It takes me a minute to focus.

I'm staring at a wall of dirt. My face resting in wet soil. I move slow. My body rages, head to toe. Yet it's cold, too. My head pounding like a subwoofer.

I hear the churn of heavy machinery. The chug of a diesel engine. Something wet, slapping and slopping.

I roll onto my back. Thin black clouds drift over a grey wash of sky, spitting for rain.

That sky looks further away than usual. I realise I'm in a hole. Big and square and high on either side.

A hole dug deep by machines, not shovels. One of those foundation pits I saw on the way in.

I peer down between my blood-stained boots. See wet cement and lots of it. It slops into the pit, out of the arse-end of a mixing truck.

I look right and see . . . A body. Wrapped in a clear plastic sheet. Naked and bleeding around the abdomen. It's a woman with long brown hair a shade darker than her skin.

I guess the plan is to bury the both of us at the same time and save on cement.

I admire their efficiency. But only for a moment. I roll onto my front, grabbing fistfuls of soil. I dig the toes of my boots into the ground. But it's slippery and hard to get traction. Harder with a broken body.

The cement keeps coming, sliding towards me.

I push up onto my forearms. Fall flat again. I'm so bloody knackered. I wanna close my eyes and sleep.

And that's exactly what I do.

But I snap out of it. Survival instinct . . . I dunno. The wet cement is cold around my ankles. It advances up my legs. I kick out. Push up. The hole filling fast.

I make it onto all fours. I hear one of the goons talking on his phone. Can't see him, but I can hear him.

I reach for my own mobile, thinking I can call the police. But my pocket's flat.

Bollocks, they took it.

I struggle to my feet. Cement around my thighs.

I see the goon talking on the phone. His back to the hole The other one must be smoking a cig somewhere. I smell it in the air.

I look for a foothold in one of the four walls of the hole, but the earth is packed tight.

Cement rises like thick porridge up my waist. As I try and twist out of it, something catches my eye. The end of a length of steel rebar, sticking out of the top of the pit on the far side. It's a good six feet away.

Can I get there? Will it even come out?

I wade in slow-motion across the pit, up to my guts. By the time I make it across, it's rising past my chest.

I reckon the hole is eight feet deep. The rebar a foot below the edge of the hole.

I'm six-five with a big wingspan. If I can force myself onto my toes and reach . . . I stretch until I get a fingertip on the rough end of the metal, leftover from a previous foundation.

I get a grip. I wiggle it left to right. It comes free from the earth—a broken metal rod, heavy and two feet in length. I grip the clean end as the cement comes up to my shoulders. A lumpy pool of the stuff filling out the pit.

Now you might be wondering why I didn't use the rebar as a grab handle and pull myself out.

Well I'm betting at least one of those two goons has a gun.

If they see me climbing out of here, what do you think they're gonna do?

Yeah, you guessed it.

But while they think I'm buried in here, they'll stay complacent. The goon on the phone'll keep yapping. His mate'll keep smoking.

And since I've buried a few bodies in this stuff, I know how it works. I stay on my tiptoes and let my weight fall backwards into the cement.

The kind of cement they're using is full of water until it sets, so it's a lot like floating to the surface of the sea. You don't fight it. You let it push you upwards.

And in no time, I'm lying on my back like a starfish,

holding the metal rod above the surface. I roll over and kick out with my legs and my spare arm. I wriggle across the sludgy grey pool, my body a few centimetres beneath the surface. My head stuck out like a crocodile approaching its prey.

I make it to the other side. The goon laughs like a drain down the phone. He's a couple of feet away from the edge of the pit, still with his back to me.

I swing the length of rebar, swiping the bastard's ankles. He yelps and drops the phone. Falls backwards and splats into the cement. He scrambles to right himself. I punch him in the face and push his head underneath before he can take a breath. He fights like hell. I hold him down. After thirty seconds, he stops struggling. I slosh a thick wave of cement over him, covering his body.

As the cement line nears the top of the hole, I dig the end of the rebar in the dirt.

I drag myself out onto the mud. I use the bar as a crutch to get to my feet. The last of the cement drips from the back of the mixer. The pit full to the edges.

I trudge towards the back of the truck. Beaten half to death. Covered head to toe in grey goo and weighing double what I did before.

Christ, it feels like I'm carrying an elephant on my back. As I rest against the passenger side of the mixing truck, I smell the cigarette again.

The driver shouts to his goon pal from the other side of the truck.

I wait.

He shouts to him again. Gets impatient and marches to the hole.

He looks around. Ditches the cig butt on the floor.

"Wazza," he shouts. "Stop fucking around. The hole's full. Time to go!"

He shakes his head and looks at the pool of cement. Something catches his eye. He walks around the hole and squats on the balls of his feet.

Shit, his dead friend's hand is sticking out of the cement.

I set off towards him, bar in hand. Dragging my right foot behind my left.

"Wazza?" the guy says, backing away from the pit.

He recognises that hand. Turns and sees me coming at him. *"What the f—"*

He reaches inside his red and black check lumberjack coat. I swing the bar and crack him in the temple. It's a heavy blow. Skims off a layer of flesh. He lurches forward, takes out the gun and lets off a round. It's way off target, his legs unsteady.

He lines up another shot. I smack the firing hand with the end of the rod. The gun spins into the cement. I swing again and hit him in the same spot on the temple. His skull cracks open. He falls backwards and splashes into the cement. I push his body down with the rebar. If you pin 'em down long enough, the cement will suck 'em beneath the surface.

I move onto Wazza's hand. I reach out and knock it down underneath.

Note to self: this rebar stuff is bloody useful.

I toss it aside and waddle over to the silver van, which I'm guessing delivered my naked companion in the pit. Both trucks are a non-starter. No way I can climb in either cab in my current state. So the van'll have to do.

The driver's door is open, but the keys must be with one of those two dead goons in the cement.

Damn, I should have thought of that.

Still, if I can climb inside I can hot-wire the thing.

But climbing is impossible when you can't raise your foot more than shin-high.

So I drag my sorry carcass inside the van, pulling myself up straight by the seat. I reach beneath the wheel and rip off the steering column panel. I slide out the pin locking the wheel and strip the wires.

I start the engine and haul my legs in one by one. I try to bend them at the knee, but I can't. So I lie on the seat, stiff and upright like a mummy. My foot on the accelerator and hands locked out on the wheel. I reach out slow and put the van in gear. I steer and shift gears like a learner driver, following the tracks out of the site. I make it through the front gate without crashing. Shit knows where I'm even going.

I pull out onto a quiet side road. It takes me a while, but I get the van going straight. Up to a T-junction.

I attempt to brake. My foot slips off the pedal. The van careers across a busy main road. A miracle I don't hit anyone. I step on the brake again too late. Unable to turn the wheel, I drive the van straight into a lamp post. Steam rises from the crumpled bonnet. I open the door and fall out onto the pavement. I limp along the road. There's a wire fence on the inside of me. A school playground full of young girls in blue jumpers. I go dizzy and fall into the wire fence.

The girls scream in horror. Shriller than dog whistles.

I guess I must look like some sort of sludge monster to them. The creature from the deep, every inch of me covered in drying cement and cuts and bruises.

There's an unlocked gate to my right. I push through it. Thinking I can rest up a minute on the other side of the fence.

I limp towards the girls. Tell 'em it's okay. I'm not gonna hurt 'em.

They hold onto each other and shriek even louder. I put a hand out to calm them down. But they must think I'm trying to grab 'em. They turn and run like hell, fighting to get in through the school doors. I start to drop in and out of consciousness. The ground spins and rushes up at me. I hit the playground and roll onto my back, a face full of sky.

As good a place to die as any.

Chapter 20

Again, I wake up.

To a freezing cold blast of something in the face.

Still not dead. Unless there's an afterlife. And it involves an old man standing over you with a hosepipe.

He sprays me in the head with the water. A crinkly little guy with a face like a skeleton, he wears dark-blue work pants, a matching polo shirt and sweater. He runs his green rubber hosepipe over me, rinsing off the cement. Must be the school caretaker. I notice the same crest on his sweater as on the wall of the school.

His eyes are dark and hollow. The ice-cold water relentless. He moves on from my head and down my body. I see the cement washing off around me. Great big pools of the stuff. My own blood mixing in, like raspberry sauce making swirls in melted ice cream.

Getting my bearings back, I see four other people stood behind the caretaker.

There's a tall man in a suit with a police badge on his hip. Hands in trouser pockets. The tails of a long, beige raincoat fanning out in a stiff breeze. Then a pair of coppers in high-vis coats and caps. And finally, a disapproving woman with curly grey hair and glasses. She looks like my old Headteacher, from the few weeks I actually went to school. Her name was Mrs Emley. I got to know her very well, the old battle axe.

The memory of her cane across my arse snaps me back to my senses.

I hear twittering birds and rustling leaves. Smell school dinners wafting from a canteen. Feel my horrible wet clothes clinging to my skin.

Next comes the pain.

Chapter 21

Amira watched in horror as the men beat Charlie to a pulp. "You're killing him!" she screamed, pounding a fist on the rear passenger window of the people carrier.

"Quiet," the driver seat said as he returned to the people carrier. "Or you'll get the same."

The arguments from Amira and Malik died down as both VW vehicles departed the building site. They exchanged nervous glances as the vans made their way through busy streets.

Ordinary life was a pane of glass away: a girl's school, a library, a Post Office and a coffee shop. Simple, everyday life, where people went to work, to school, to meet with a friend over a slice of cake.

Yet it felt a thousand miles away. She may as well have been at the start of her journey, when she first packed her bag in Aleppo. The same bag a thief would later snatch from her on a crowded market street in Turkey.

Amira's people carrier followed the other. One way traffic turned into a dual carriageway, which turned into a long stretch of motorway. A sweeping A-road followed, into a country road flanked by fields of grazing cattle.

At least Rima was in good hands. That was something. Though it didn't stop her worrying about the fate of the young girl.

The driver turned onto a narrow lane running beneath a canopy of overhanging trees. They appeared black against the light grey sky. An ominous sign.

The people carriers came to a stop in front of a high wall with barbed wire on top. A dark-green steel gate slid open and they continued through.

Were these people with the military? Was all this government sponsored?

The sight of a plainclothes guard on the gate seemed to suggest not. He carried an automatic weapon strapped over one shoulder. A cigarette between finger and thumb.

The driver wound down his window and yelled something at the guard. He spoke in what sounded like Eastern European. The guard gave the driver the finger in return. The driver laughed.

A wide concrete training yard led up to a large, brown-brick building.

The place looked abandoned. It sat behind an unkempt grass bank, paint peeling off the white window frames and a flagpole missing a flag.

"What is this place?" Amira said, thinking out loud.

"An old army barracks," Malik said.

"What do you think we're doing here?" Amira asked.

"Who knows," Malik said.

The driver brought the people carrier to a stop outside the building. He got out and slid open the rear door. "Out," he said.

Amira and the others lined up on the tarmac, as if they were recruits fresh off an army bus.

The drivers held them at gunpoint until another guard opened a fire exit door. He waved them in. The drivers pushed and shoved the passengers along a stone path that led up the grass bank.

Out of the blue, one of the passengers made a break for freedom. A gangly Somali man with overgrown stubble and panic in his eyes. He peeled off the line and sprinted towards the nearest people carrier, as if planning to steal it.

"What are you doing?" Malik said under his breath.

The drivers looked on in curiosity. They laughed as the guard holding the door open spoke into a small radio on the collar of his blue tracksuit top.

Amira watched as the man opened the driver's door to the people carrier. Finding no key in the ignition, he whirled around and made a run for the entrance. He shrunk into the distance, approaching the guard on the front gate.

The guard seemed unconcerned, smoking his cigarette. With the merest of efforts, he lifted the barrel of his rifle and let off a quick burst of fire.

Immune to such things, no one standing in line flinched at the sight and sound of a gun. Yet there were gasps as the man fell to the ground, face down on the tarmac. Even from a distance, blood could be seen from his wounds.

The man who'd driven Amira and Malik to the barracks

spat on the ground. "Come on," he said. "Inside."

Marched at gunpoint, the line filtered into the building. It was dark and dank. The air stale and the permanent dripping of a pipe echoing down long, dingy corridors.

Amira walked towards the back of the line, through two sets of heavy oak doors. The guard leading the refugees stopped in his tracks. He told everyone to line up against a wall to the left.

For a moment, Amira thought they were going to execute each refugee, one by one. She stood with her back against the wall, trembling in fear—not the only one. They'd taken their money, passports and valuables—now they would kill them and dispose of the bodies.

Amira pictured a handgun to the head for a quick, clean kill. Suddenly, death in Syria seemed like a comfort. She imagined the scene: reclining in an armchair, listening to music and drinking tea. A mortar shell drops through the ceiling. She doesn't even see it coming. It would have been an acceptable fate.

But not here, not like this.

The lead guard handed his rifle to another member of the gang. He reached inside his jacket for his handgun.

Chapter 22

I don't know why I keep pulling at this bastard handcuff. It's not coming off. And the bedrail it's attached too won't budge either. Not because it's especially sturdy. It's just that I'm so bloody weak.

I look around the ward, the bed propped up forty-five degrees. There's an old man with a broken leg, elevated in a sling. A young guy who looks like he's been in a car wreck: head wrapped in bandages and arm set in plaster. Another middle-aged bloke on a drip with a post-op dressing on his throat.

Then there's me. Hooked up to a catheter bag

It's not that I can't piss. The nurses say I can't walk far enough to the toilet.

Here comes one of 'em now.

"Nurse," I say, rattling the cuff against the bed rail. "Any chance of a mirror?"

She's a short, tubby blonde with the bedside manner of a caged gorilla. She plants her hands on her hips. "Do I look like your personal slave?"

"Just so I can see the damage."

She tuts and takes a clipboard off the end of the bed. "Let's see, you've got a fractured skull, two broken ribs, multiple lacerations and several deep muscle contusions."

"But other than that, I'm fine."

She pauses and frowns at me. "You look like you've been to death and back."

"I'm out of the woods though. You can take off the piss bag and the cuffs."

She laughs and shuffles on her way. "Fat chance."

Southern cow. I reach for a plastic cup of water on a table to my right. I'm hit by daggers of pain in my ribs, my back, my skull. Every bloody body part you can think of.

I stretch through the pain and grab the cup. Take a drink. The more I move, the faster I'll recover. No matter what the docs tell you, that's the secret. I've been through enough beatings to know.

I sit up straight in bed and get a better look along the ward. There's a pig in uniform guarding the entrance. He sits on a chair with his back to me.

Beyond him, I catch sight of a detective marching up the corridor. I can tell he's a copper from here. It's a sixth sense I've got. This one's a lanky bastard with floppy, sandy hair. A flat face with small features and eyes loitering close to a slim, freckled nose.

In his early forties, I reckon. He looks older the closer he gets, striding up to the end of the bed and putting on the brakes.

He takes a good look at me. "Charles Cobb?" he asks in

a Home Counties accent. Posher than cockney, but still with a twang of London.

"I might be." I say.

He moves around the bed. Stands over me, hands in pockets. I realise he's the guy from the schoolyard. The same face. The same clothes. "I'm Detective Clarke, National Crime Agency."

"Oh great," I say. "What are you here to finger me for, the stuff up north or the stuff down here?"

"Can't say I care about your previous activities," says Clarke, taking a card from a grey trouser pocket. He hands it over. "Though I thought a man in your position would be keeping a low profile. What with all that bother in Manchester."

"I am . . . Or I was. I've gone straight."

"Well that's obvious," he says.

"How was I to know there were people in the back of that truck? They told me I was shifting goods."

"Well, one way or another, you've got yourself in a right mess. You're facing a lengthy stretch."

I hand back the card. "I know where this is going. What do you want?"

"The name of your contact would be a start. Who hired you?"

"Funny, I don't remember," I say. "Must be the skull fracture."

"You're gonna protect the guy?" Clarke says. "After the state they left you in?"

"Look, I don't grass," I say. "Even if I did know the bloke's name . . . Which I don't."

Clarke sags in the shoulders and shakes his head.

A woman hurries in with a green cardboard file under her arm. She's younger than Clarke with olive skin, but in the same brand of sober suit all these detectives wear. Her dark hair tied tight to her head. "Sorry guv," she says to Clarke. "Parking was a nightmare." She hands him the file and looks at me. "This the driver of the truck?"

"This is our man," Clarke says. "But surprise, surprise, he doesn't wanna snitch."

"Why should I?" It's not like you're gonna let me go."

"I've seen your record," Clarke says. "You're a career criminal. But not *that* kind of criminal."

"Can I have that in English?"

"You're not a trafficker," the female detective says.

"Charlie, this is Detective Morales," Clarke says. "She's working with me on a case we've been building for some time now."

"A case on what?"

"The people who did that to you," Morales says, pointing to my bruised and battered face.

"Well you're not getting very far," I say. "They've got a right little industry going. They're bringing these people in by the truckload. Thousands a pop. Can't say I agree with it."

"Then give us a name," Clarke says.

"Newsflash pal. Me and the law don't exactly get along. Why would I help you?"

"You don't care about the people you helped smuggle into the country?" Morales asks.

"They got in. They'll be set up with houses. Jobs. So what? I don't give a shit who you chuck out of the country."

Clarke opens the file. He spreads a few photos out on the bed. Grainy pictures of grim-looking digs behind barbed wire fences. "They keep them in secure compounds, under lock and key."

"And at gunpoint," Morales says.

"The people you've been working for are much more than smugglers," Clarke says.

"Yeah, I got that impression," I say, wincing as I move.

"These men run a slave ring," Morales says, tapping one of the photos. "They make money off the smuggle, then crowd them into compounds."

"Disgusting places," Clarke says. "No heating or running water."

"They feed them rations and force them to work for nothing," Morales says. "Fields and factories . . . if they're lucky."

"Worse if they're young, attractive and female," Clarke says.

"Or the traffickers are after a few organs to sell," says Morales. She parks her arse on the edge of the bed. "If anyone refuses, they threaten to send them back to where they came from."

"If they're caught escaping—" Clarke says, running a thumb across his throat.

I take a sip of water. "If you know all this already, why do you need me? Why not raid these shit-holes? Make some arrests?"

"The law's not as simple as that," Clarke says.

"The only information we've got is the testimony of an escaped migrant," says Morales. "Whoever's running the shop stays well out of sight."

"And we suspect they might have someone inside the force, tipping them off," Clarke says.

"Every raid has come up empty," says Morales.

"I'm not surprised," I say. "These lads are proper pros. You won't get near 'em."

"That's why we need you to give us a name," Clarke says. "A bit of traction. A foot in the door."

I think about Amira and the others, stripped of their money, their stuff, their dignity. Forced to work and left to rot. "How long have you been after these arseholes?" I ask.

"It's ongoing," Clarke says, "But this particular case . . . Four, maybe five years?"

"Then I'll make you a deal," I say, seeing a window of opportunity. My ribs catch fire as I lean forward. "Give me what you've got and turn me loose on 'em. I'll do more in an afternoon than you lot could do in another five years."

Morales laughs. "Come on, look at you."

"They caught me by surprise, that's all. I'll be right as rain in a few days." I cough up some blood as I say it. I swallow it down. "If you're so bloody familiar with my record, you'll know this is what I do."

"Oh, and what do you get in return?" Morales asks. She seems amused by the idea.

"I give you the people who are doing this. You let me walk."

"If you *could* walk," Clarke says.

Morales shakes her head. "You must think we came down in the last shower."

Clarke sighs and looks at Morales, then at me. He gathers the photos together inside the file and closes it. He fastens the file with two large paperclips over the top. "Tempting as your offer might be, Charlie, I don't have the authority to sanction that."

"It was worth a try," I say with a shrug. Damn, shrugging hurts too.

Clarke rests the file on my bedside table. He leaves his card, too. "Think it over," he says, tapping the card. "Give me a call when you're ready to talk." As they turn to leave, Clarke stops mid-stride. "Oh, and in case you're thinking of doing a runner, we've got an armed guard out there. Six-hour shifts around the clock."

The detectives walk out of the ward. I rest back against the bed. I glance at the file on the table. At the paper clips fixed on top.

Chapter 23

They finally take the piss bag off me. The narky blonde nurse does it. And she's not the delicate type. She pulls the catheter out of my chap: more painful than a kick in the bollocks with a steel boot.

"Oh, don't be such a softie," the nurse says.

I'm about to say something back when I see the police guard giving me the eyeballs.

He stands at the side of the bed.

"You enjoying this mate?" I ask him.

"A little bit, yeah," the smirking shit-bag says.

I pull at the cuff on my right wrist. "Do the honours will you? I need to get out of this bed."

"Don't get any ideas," he says, removing the cuff.

"Does it look like I'm going anywhere?" I say, easing myself out of bed. I put both feet on the floor, rising with the help of the bed rail.

The copper removes the handcuff. He strolls slow behind me as I stagger round the ward. I down a jug of water and go for a proper slash. Holy shit, the burn. The nurse didn't warn me about the burn.

I cry out in pain.

The copper thumps on the other side of the toilet door. "Everything okay in there?"

"What do you think, dickhead? I'm pissing razor blades here."

"Good," the copper says. "Just wanted to make sure."

"Yeah, yeah. You're loving it now. But you won't be when I make my move and your head's on your sergeant's chopping block."

I hear him sniggering behind the door. "Dream on you sack of shit."

I emerge from the toilet and head back to bed, every step unsteady, body wanting to collapse and sleep. But I wanna get it used to moving again. ASAP. I force myself to stretch before I get back in bed. It's brutal, but good for the joints.

Day two in hospital and they serve me up some food. I *say* food: a defrosted square of white fish with some white jizz on top. A handful of tiny cubed potatoes and carrots they didn't even bother pulling the roots out of. I push the plate away.

"You've got to eat something," the nurse says. "It's good for you."

"They once said that about cigarettes."

"You won't get your pudding," she says.

"Thank Christ for that," I say, handing her the plate.

"You know, you won't recover if you don't eat," she says, expressing her complete lack of knowledge of how these meat-suits of ours work.

See, when you've spent half your adult life extracting information out of people, it pays to learn a thing or two about the human body.

Pudding and square potato bits are full of sugar. So's the jizz sauce. And the last thing you need is sugar.

Besides, the body heals much quicker in a fasted state. Spiking your blood sugars only increases inflammation. And when your body's trying to digest food, it's not healing fractures and cuts and fighting infection.

So I ignore the rumbling in my belly and the nonsense spouted by the nurse. I continue to refuse food the rest of the day and focus on chugging more of that water.

The water flushes the burn out of the old chap and the toilet trips loosen me up a little each time.

I go to sleep early. I wake up at nine the next morning. Breakfast is bacon and scrambled eggs, which is fine. High fat, low sugar. The preferred energy source of the brain and body. I wolf it down. Not 'cause I can't wait to eat it, but 'cause I don't wanna taste it.

I nod off for an hour after brekkie. When I wake up, Cassie, and her mother, Mandy, are sitting next to the bed.

"What are you two doing here?" I ask.

"Hello to you, too," Mandy says, pulling a face. She wears tight blue jeans with rips in 'em. A pink top under the same leather jacket she's had for twenty years. And her dirty blonde hair pinned up, which makes her face look older. Not that I'd ever dare say it.

"You okay, Dad?" Cassie asks in a frayed blue jumper, sleeves pulled over hands. Light blonde hair styled messy as usual. Her blue eyes welling up as she stands up and looks over me.

"Never better," I say. "Why are you here and not studying?"

"Why are you in a hospital bed?" she says, glancing at the file Detective Clarke left on the side table. "What are they gonna do to them?"

"The immigrants?"

"Asylum seekers, Dad," Cassie says. She chews her lip. Deep in thought. She stands and picks up the file. Flicks through and shakes her head. Sad Bambi eyes staring at the photos. "Those poor people. You should do something."

"What am I? The Bleeding Heart Foundation? Besides . . . "I rattle the handcuff against the bed rail.

Mandy folds her arms and pulls a face at me.

"Okay, I'll *think* about looking into it. In a few weeks. Once I get rested."

"They haven't got weeks," Cassie says.

Christ, since Cassie hit university age, these two have become like a bloody tag team.

"Listen Cass, chances are I'll be in a prison cell. Not much I can do when I'm under arrest—"

"Who are you talking to?" the copper guarding me asks. It's a different one this time. Shorter and wider. With his rose-red cheeks and a shaved head, he looks like an overgrown choirboy.

The guest chair by the side of the bed is empty. The file exactly where Clarke left it on the table. Cassie and Mandy nowhere to be seen.

Shit. Having imaginary conversations. Always one of those two, or a combination of both. I need to try and realise when it's happening. But the extra bangs in the head are hardly gonna help. A baseball bat to the skull is what triggered 'em in the first place.

Still, imaginary or not, Cassie might have a point. I grab the file from the bedside table and open it up. I'm not much of a reader, so I flip through the papers, looking at the pictures and scanning the key info.

As I do, the image of Amira forced into slavery invades my head. I snap the file shut and dump it on the bedside table.

The guard sets off back to his post at the end of the ward.

"Hey," I say. "Couldn't get them to bring my clothes, could you?" He eyes me with suspicion. "I wanna feel human again. I'd rather be in the nick than here." I can see the pig isn't budging. He's a real by-the-book type. "Look pal, the sooner I'm back on my feet and behind bars, the sooner they'll pull you off babysitting duty."

He looks around the ward. Mumbles under his breath. "I *do* hate hospitals."

Half an hour later, he comes up with the goods. A porter drops off my laundered clothes in a white plastic bag. The copper removes the cuff from my wrist and escorts me to the toilet.

I'm walking better now. Stiff as hell but steady. I get changed in the toilet. It's hard work. Especially pulling my jeans on and my t-shirt over my head.

I look in the mirror. The swelling above my left eye is

going down. My cuts are beginning to scab and my bruises are yellowing out already.

See, what did I tell you? Fasting, water and high-fat meals. Works wonders. Next time you take a beating, follow Dr Breaker's advice.

Though, having said that, it's not all sunshine and rainbows. My limp is still there and my open fracture will take weeks to fully heal.

The copper walks me back to the bed. I leave my boots and jacket in the bag on the floor. I sit in bed and watch the TV. Twenty-four-seven news. It has the time on the bottom-right of the screen. I watch the hours tick by until 2pm.

That's it. I've been watching 'em change every six hours. One guy comes and the other leaves. The new guy always arrives with food: a flask of coffee, a packed lunch and a newspaper. Sometimes a donut, a McDonalds or Subway bag. They'll settle down on a chair outside for an hour or so. They'll drink the coffee and scoff their food and then after a while they'll need a piss or a shit.

That leaves me at least two minutes while they walk along the ward to the nearest toilet. An hour in, the latest chap decides he can't hold it any longer. He shuffles past the bed, casts an eye over me. I'm in my clothes, but my hand is still cuffed. I pretend I'm snoozing in front of the TV, but from the slit of one eye, I watch him waddle off. Yeah, that's the walk of a man who needs to drop off a couple of kids. And he's got his paper in hand, too.

I open my eyes and sit up in bed. I've got the paperclips from the file bent into shape and ready in my hand. While no one's looking, I use them to pick the lock on the cuff. A piece of piss when you've done it a thousand times.

I'm out in seconds. I slip off the bed and into my boots. I grab my jacket, the file and Detective Clarke's card. I hobble along the ward and out into a mile of corridor.

I've gotta get to the end before that copper returns from the toilet. I reckon I've got five minutes tops to make it out of the building before he returns.

All he'll find is an empty bed and a set of cuffs dangling off the rail, but I can't get complacent. I slip my bomber jacket on as I walk. Pain shooting in all directions as I force my arms in the sleeves. I fold Clarke's file over lengthways and stuff it in my inside jacket pocket. I zip up and keep moving. At one point I'm in a race with a pensioner working a zimmer frame. That's how slow I am. But I round the corner. One step closer to freedom.

Shit.

Another long stretch of white walls and grey lino. There are lifts at the end, but I hear shouts echoing down the corridor, coming from behind me.

The copper's voice bounces off the walls. "Anyone seen a big guy? Six-five. Cuts and bruises."

I speed up as best I can. The lifts another twenty feet away. I hear police-issue boots running after me.

Think, Charlie, think.

Chapter 24

I see an opportunity to my right. A private room. I try the door and it opens. No one inside. Just an empty hospital bed and a gurney parked up alongside it. A dead body on top under a white sheet. The bed is made and there are daffodils in a nearby bin. I close the door behind me and flatten against the wall. Through a narrow pane of glass in the door I see the copper run past, yapping into his radio. He's heading for the lifts. They'll have this place locked down in no time.

I look at the person-shaped bump under the sheet. Can't be too long before a porter comes and collects the poor sod. I lurch over to the gurney and whip off the sheet. It's an old man with a naval tattoo on his forearm. I throw the sheet aside and haul him off the gurney by the armpits, his skin ice-cold to the touch.

His feet make a slapping sound as they hit the floor. I pull him backwards around the far side of the bed. I set him down on the floor, hidden from sight from anyone entering the room.

Yeah, yeah, I know it's wrong. But needs must. And anyway, he was in the Navy. He'd of understood, right?

I return to the gurney, grab the sheet and park my arse on the edge. I swing my legs up and pull the sheet over my lower half. I lie flat and drape the top of the sheet over my head.

I lie still, waiting for the porter. I could be here for hours, but I'm not ready to run or fight yet. This is my only chance.

As I'm lying there, I hear feet running to and fro along the corridor. Coppers searching the floor.

"I'll check in here," one of 'em says.

I hear the door handle click open. I hold my breath. My heart pounding in my chest. It seems an age, but I hear him leave. He closes the door and tells some other pig the room's all clear.

"Must be on another floor," his copper mate says.

The police toddle off and all goes quiet again. I breathe a sigh of relief, rippling the cotton sheet over my face. After a few minutes, I feel a warm body lying tight up next to me. The smell of aloe vera. Did I fall asleep? No. My eyes are wide open.

Cassie jabs a finger in my chest. "Can't believe you just did that."

"What?" I whisper back.

"Dragged that man over there and left him on the floor. He's only just died."

"He won't mind. He's making himself useful."

"It's messed up."

"Yeah, well it's a messed-up world. You'll come to find that out when you—"

"Shush, Dad, someone's coming."

"What do you mean, shush? You sh—Cassie?"

And like that's she's gone again. I wonder if there's a new drug for these hallucinations. Something that doesn't make me want to throw up and kill myself like the ones I stopped taking. Much as it's great to see my only child, it's not the same as the real thing.

I hold my breath again. The door opens and a pair of feet enter the room. I see a shadow loom over the sheet. The gurney starts moving and turning, until we're out in the corridor.

The porter has a foreign accent. Italian? He talks to himself. "God, this one's heavy."

I let a soft breath out of the corner of my mouth. Shallow enough so it doesn't ripple the sheet. The gurney wheels squeak all the way along the corridor.

"Hey, stop," a booming voice says.

The porter puts on the brakes. "Can I help you officer?" he says.

The copper is close. I can tell by the smell of bacon. I hold my breath again and make a fist with my right hand. Hopefully I can still swing my arm.

"You seen a big ugly guy in black?"

Ugly? The cheeky—

"No," the porter says. "Why?"

"He's a fugitive. If you see him, he's dangerous. So don't approach him. Call security."

"Um, okay," the porter says. "Good luck."

The gurney moves. Not long before we stop again. I hear

a lift door ping open. The porter wheels me in. Spins me round one-eighty. The lift door closes.

"Going down," a robotic female voice says. The lift stops and starts a couple of times, but no one seems to be getting in.

"I'll catch the next one," I hear a woman say.

Can't blame 'em. No one wants to stand next to a dead body in a confined space.

The robot woman counts us down to the basement level.

I think it's safe to say we're headed to the hospital morgue. I should be okay from here, so I throw off the sheet and sit bolt upright.

The porter jumps out of his skin. Screams in terror. Makes a cross with his finger. He's a wiry little goateed man in spinach-green scrubs. Actually, he might be Greek. I dunno. He grips a silver cross around his neck for dear life.

"Come on," I say. "You never seen a talking dead bloke?"

It seems to dawn on him that I'm the fugitive. That I'm dangerous. The lift opens. I haul him to his feet by the arm.

"Where's the nearest exit?" I ask.

The porter directs me to a set of stairs. "Two floors up there's a door out back. But you'll need—"

"One of these?" I say, swiping his ID card off his hip. "Cheers pal."

I climb the stairs. Far more painful than walking straight. But I find a discreet white door at the top of the second flight. I swipe out onto a quiet road that runs along the rear of the main building. As I toss the ID card in a bin, a little yellow bus stops close by. I climb on-board with a few others and take a seat halfway along on the right.

The doors close and the bus takes off. As we trundle away from the hospital, the cavalry speeds past us the opposite way. A train of three police cars. Lights and sirens going berserk.

"What do you think all that's about?" an old Caribbean man asks me, over his shoulder.

I shrug, Detective Clarke's file on my lap. "Beats me."

Chapter 25

Like most things, the bathtub in my bedsit is too small for my body. If I lie down, my legs stick out of the water. If I sit up, only my legs fit in. It's old too, with a permanent black ring around the middle that no amount of scrubbing is getting off.

I start with a cold bath. I run the tap the coldest it'll go, fill her up and dump in two bags of ice cubes I bought from the local supermarket.

I remove my clothes. Everything aching. I look at the ice floating on the surface of the water. Psyche myself up, hook a leg over and plant a foot in the water.

Christ, it's freezing. *What the hell am I doing?*

Nothing I haven't done before.

I climb in and squat over the surface. Have to do it fast. If you lower in slow, the ice water plays merry hell with your balls.

I count to three and dunk myself in, lying low so it's up to my neck. My knees stick a mile out of the tub. I gasp at the cold. Shiver for a few minutes until I get used to it.

It numbs the pain in my body. I take a deep breath and slide lower, submerging fully. I watch tiny little icebergs floating above my head. I count to thirty and pop back out of the water.

I stay in the bath for ten minutes before clambering out. I wrap myself in a towel. The inflammation in my body easing off already. My mind three times more awake.

I let the ice water drain and run a hot bath in its place. I climb in again and repeat the process, letting head and body soak in the steaming water.

This one's for relaxation. It loosens up the joints and muscles.

The hot and cold is good for the immune system, too. Gets your blood pumping and speeds up healing. I lie in the bath with Ducky, my yellow rubber duck, bobbing on the surface. I've had Ducky since I was two. He goes everywhere I go. And I don't bathe without him.

Sometimes I talk to Ducky. I run things past him. Problems. Decisions. Peeves.

As I'm bouncing a few thoughts off him, I hear a tinkling sound. I smell the end of a cigarette burning. I look up to my left.

It's Mandy. Sat on my toilet, smoking one of her twenty a day.

"Ten," she says. "I cut down."

Mandy takes another drag. The bathroom is so small, she's almost on top of me, in the clothes she wore at the hospital. Her jeans and knickers around her ankles.

"You still talking to that thing?" she says, looking at

Ducky. She tuts and takes another drag. Looks at a glossy photo in her spare hand. Straight from the file Detective Clarke left me.

"What are you doing with that?" I ask.

"More importantly, what are you gonna do next?" she says.

"Get out of London, that's what."

Mandy raises her eyebrows. Lets out a cloud of smoke.

"So they beat me half to death. You can't take it personally Mand. Not in this business."

"So you're still *in* the business."

"I didn't say that."

"So much for *making a positive difference.*" She air quotes me as she says it. I hate it when people do that. "Didn't last long, did it?" she says.

Mandy looks at the photograph. I angle my head to see. A long lens snap of that compound the detectives were on about.

"Alright," I say. "So Clarke may have left me the paper clips on purpose. He may have even clued me in on the shift changes of the guards. But that doesn't mean I'm off the hook. My best bet is to skip town. Start again."

The steam rises off the water. The tap at the end of the bath drips. I look at Mandy. At Ducky. Mandy smokes and gazes at the photo. Ducky stares at me with his big black eyes. Until I can't take it any longer.

I sit up fast in the bath. "Alright, alright. I'll do something. Just stop going on about it, the pair of you." I climb out of the bath. "Thanks a lot, Ducky."

Mandy covers her eyes and screws up her mouth. "Oh, warn me next time, Charlie."

I step onto the floor. Water dripping on the dirty lino. "Nothing you haven't seen before. Now pass me a towel."

Mandy doesn't answer. She's gone. The photo too. I grab a bright blue towel off the railing and wrap it around my bruised body. I dry myself off, muscles loosening up by the minute. I brush my teeth and pull on some fresh clothes. I look in the bathroom mirror.

Like I said, I'm not angry about Randall stiffing me over. Hell, it'd be a bit rich if I was. I've handed enough beatings out of my own. But the more I think about what they're doing to those refugees . . . They're ordinary people getting buggered from every angle. It grinds my bloody gears.

I look at Ducky. "You're right. I should call her."

I pad into the living room and pick my new pay-as-you-go handset off the sofa. I dial the number of the burner I handed to Amira.

The call picks up on the other end to a scuffle. I hear shouts, screams, words in a foreign language. The line goes quiet.

"Who is this?" I ask.

No answer. Just breathing.

"Who the fuck are you?" I ask again.

The line clicks and goes dead. Ducky's right. Someone needs to do something.

Chapter 26

The guard's weapon of choice was a camera. A small, silver camera he pulled from inside a jacket pocket. He struggled to work it in chunky, dirty fingers. After some discussion with the other two men, he appeared to get to grips with the camera. He motioned to the line of refugees to stand up straight and clicked one rapid shot after another.

The flash left spots in Amira's eyes. The three men walked up and down the line, debating an issue in their own language. The lead guard then strode off along the corridor. He disappeared through a large set of doors signed *Gym Hall*.

Ten, tense minutes later, he returned with stapled sheets of print paper. Amira caught a glimpse: a headshot of each refugee and number alongside each photograph.

They appeared to be consulting the sheets and comparing them to the people in line. The guard pointed at different faces, while the drivers pulled them out of line. They positioned them either to the left or the right.

Most of the group stood to the left, mostly men. The

group to the right consisted of three women. The younger women. Amira was the last one remaining. The lead guard pushed her to the right. She joined a young black woman who appeared Somali or Eritrean. Another she'd spoken to, from Syria and the third, from Afghanistan, Malik had told her.

The guard led the larger group towards the Gym Hall.

The two drivers harried and hassled Amira's group back out to the people carrier she'd arrived in. As they walked, Amira felt the phone Charlie had given her vibrate. It played a jaunty tune. She dug it out of her pocket fast—fumbled with the buttons to answer the call. Before she could shout for help, one of the drivers wrestled it out of her hands. She cried out, hoping the person on the other end would hear. The driver shoved her away and listened in silence. After a brief pause, he cut off the call.

Could it have been Charlie? Surely not. She'd seen him beaten to death . . . *The British police, then?*

It mattered little now. She was ordered inside the people carrier with the other women. Both drivers took their seats up front. The burner phone deposited in the glove box.

As they passed through the barrack gates, Amira clung to the faint hope that the men had decided to let them go.

It disintegrated entirely when a long journey ended at a dock. It ran alongside a vast stretch of water, the London Eye, Big Ben and the Houses of Parliament in the far distance.

The dock was busy with freight ships, warehouses and stacked, seawater-stained shipping containers. The driver stopped alongside a long white cargo ship with a bright blue hull.

He turned and watched Amira and the girls. The man in the passenger seat opened the slide door and took the African woman by the arm. He slid the door shut and led her a few feet across the dock to a narrow set of white steps. He pushed her up the steps with his gun dug into her back.

They disappeared through a doorway on deck. The man returned alone and repeated the process until Amira was the only one left. He reappeared and grabbed her by the arm. He dragged her out onto the dock. Amira spotted a pair of workers in high visibility orange, talking further up the road. She yelled for help with all the voice she had.

The workers turned, looked for a moment, then resumed their conversation.

The driver forced a hand over Amira's mouth. He marched her up the stairs, his grip too strong for her to wriggle free. Within seconds, she was inside—the steel door to the ship closed and the driver gone.

Another man took over, dressed like a dock worker—a big navy coat and woolly hat, black boots and trousers.

He manhandled Amira down a metal staircase. Along a claustrophobic corridor that smelled of engine oil. Down another set of stairs and another corridor, indistinct from the last.

They kept walking until they came to a large cargo hold lit a dull red. A long, high room made of solid steel. There were two long rows of cubicles. They ran either side of the hold—single beds partitioned by blue hospital curtains.

The stench got to Amira first: sweat, sex and sickness. Then the sight of girls lying on unmade beds, drips in their arms. Their skin pale and movements woozy.

Amira noticed a nearby curtain half-drawn. The mudded grips of a man's boots hanging over the end of a bed, his trousers around his ankles. The bed squeaking as his feet moved back and forth.

The guard pushed Amira into the room, his accent local. "Come on darlin', let's find you a bed."

He marched Amira down the aisle to a cubicle on the left. The curtain was open. He forced her to sit on the end of the bed. He stood over her, unbuckling his belt. "I'll give you a try out first."

"Here," Amira said, "let me."

The guard seemed surprised. "That's the spirit," he said, letting her take over.

Amira pushed his trousers down around his shins.

"Like a bit of meat, do yer?" he said. "Yeah, I bet you do over there, don't yer?"

Amira looked up and smiled at the guard. She put a hand on the tail of his coat. The guard ran his tongue under his bottom lip. "Go on darlin', say *ah*."

Amira rose fast off the bed, driving a knee into the guard's testicles. He reeled away in pain, ankles caught in the legs of his trousers. Falling backwards, he hit his head on the solid steel edge of the bed behind. Blood seeped out from the back of the man's skull. Amira ran her hands over his torso and found a handgun next to his ribs. She ran out of the cargo hold and along corridors, searching breathless for an exit.

Right turns. Left turns. She couldn't remember which way they'd come.

Then she spotted it. The staircase to the upper decks. High on adrenaline, she sprinted up it and ran for the next one. She saw it ahead, at the end of the corridor.

She sensed freedom at last. All she had to do was make it up those stairs and out off the deck. She'd raise the alarm, gladly handing herself over to the authorities. They could do what they wanted with her—deport her for all she cared.

But she *had* to make it out.

As she flew towards the staircase, a figure appeared from a doorway to the right. There was no time to stop, swerve, or use the gun. He grabbed hold of her and snatched the weapon from her hand.

"Where are you going, my dear?" He spoke in English. A gentle European voice. His grip firm but not fierce. A handsome man with long, greying hair, glasses and stubble. Dressed in a tailored, dark-blue suit, he stood out from the rest.

Another man appeared in the doorway, again clothed as if working on the docks. He was shorter, with receding hair and dark skin. To Amira, he looked Moroccan or Algerian.

"Who have we got here?" the suited man asked him.

The other man consulted a clipboard. "She just got in," he said in a different accent. Definitely not English. "She's one of the cargo girls," he continued. "I'll have her straightened out."

"No, no, no," the dapper man said. "There's no need for that." He handed the smaller man the gun and smiled at Amira. "You look tired my dear. Come in and take a seat."

He guided her through the doorway, into a small office. There was a desk and three visitor chairs to the immediate left. He sat her down on the middle chair. "My name's Pavel," he said. "What's yours?"

Amira didn't speak.

"Are you thirsty? Would you like a drink? Tea? Coffee?"

"Water," Amira found herself mumbling.

"Coming right up," Pavel said, filling a clear plastic cup from a water cooler in the far corner.

The smaller man dropped into a chair behind the desk, appearing as confused as Amira.

Pavel handed over the cup of water to Amira. Her hand shook as she raised it to her lips.

"Here," Pavel said, steadying her hand, helping her to drink.

She finished the cup in one go, recovering her breath.

"What do you want to do with her?" the man behind the desk asked. "We're a girl short as it is."

Pavel took a seat next to Amira. He removed his glasses. He pulled a silk, navy handkerchief from a trouser pocket and rubbed the lenses. "We can get another," he said. "This one's special."

"Yeah, she's pretty, but—"

"No, she's beautiful," Pavel said, slipping on his glasses. "Under all this dirt . . . And she's got fight. Guts. I like that." Pavel toyed with a strand of Amira's hair. Amira flinched away. Pavel held up a hand in apology.

"Fine," the man behind the desk said, "I'll order a replacement. But we can't throw her out on the street. You want her sending back to the barracks?" He picked up the receiver on an office phone. "I can tell Sergei to turn around—"

"No, no," Pavel said, his gaze fixed on Amira. "She's coming with me." Pavel stood from his chair. He held out a hand for Amira to take. He was polite, sophisticated. But he was one of them.

"What about the other women?" Amira asked. "What happens to them?"

"I would take them all if I could," Pavel said. "But it's Nabil's boat."

Amira didn't believe him. Didn't trust him. Regardless, she took his hand.

Chapter 27

I use the walk to the Old Ship to stretch my legs. By the time I get there, I'm back to my usual loping stride. I enter the pub at nine. The place is busy with the after-work crowd. And not the office kind. We're talking labourers in dusty boots and t-shirts. Middle-aged men with beer bellies in polo shirts. The odd woman caked in makeup and wearing clothes that used to fit 'em when they were younger. They used to be in fashion, too.

I shoulder my way to the front of the bar, ignoring the funny looks I get on the way. The landlord is on duty again, wearing the same England shirt. He pours me a pint. I sup on the head.

Wow that tastes good.

Everything tastes good when you've come back from the dead. Even watered-down piss like this. I turn and look around the pub. I notice a bunch of guys in the far corner, gathered around a table. They stop talking and stare my way. They're in their forties and fifties, ugly as a hat full of arseholes.

I move around the pub. I tap a few blokes on the shoulder and ask 'em if Randall's been in. They shake their heads and say no. That means they're not part of his outfit. If they were, they'd act dumb and pretend they didn't know him.

I save the table of mean-looking dickheads until last.

"What the fuck do you want?" a thickset man with cropped ginger hair asks me.

"You seen Chris Randall?" I ask. "Expecting him in tonight?"

A bloke with a pock face and an uneven black goatee levels me in the eye. "Don't know who you're talking about mate, but you'd better stop talking. Kapeesh?"

"Easy Captain Sparrow," I say, "Only asking."

"Well don't," the ginger one says.

I sink the last quarter of my pint. I dump the glass on their table and back away, glancing over a shoulder in case I'm done from behind.

I leave the warmth of the pub for the dark, chilly London streets. A light fog hanging in the air, softening the glare of oncoming headlights.

I head back to the bedsit. Around halfway home, where the streets are residential and empty, I notice a tail behind me. On foot. Hanging back, but definitely following me. A car too. Driving slow around the area. Cruising by me three separate times.

There's a couple more pubs on the way home. Even rougher than the Old Ship. There's also a couple of takeaway joints, a corner shop and a tiny chippy with wire mesh over the windows.

I stop inside and order fish, chips and mushy peas, plus

a pot of ketchup and a can of coke. I come out of the chippy and leave the housing estates for the tower blocks. The same bloke is still on my tail. The mystery car parked up across the street.

There's a smell of burning in the air. I notice a car on fire in the distance. Shrieks and shouts in the fog. As I reach the entrance to my tower block, I stop and turn. My tail has disappeared. No sign of the car either.

The gang who hang around the base of the apartments are out for the night, causing bother somewhere else. I head up to my bedsit. Check over my shoulder again as I wrestle my way in through the front door. I lock the door behind me. I take a fork off the drainer and slip out of my jacket. I drop onto the sofa, turn on the TV and open out the bundle of chip paper on a tiny wooden coffee table. I fizz open the coke, dump the ketchup on the chips and dig in.

You can't beat fish and chips. Even the bad ones are good. And the local chippy isn't bad. I'm not long into the chips when I hear the sound of feet outside the front door. I see the lock turning. Hear whatever tool they're using to open it, jiggling around.

I turn up the TV and get up from the sofa. I tiptoe over to the door. Stand on the inside of it, back to the wall. Canned laughter blares out of the TV. One of those crappy panel shows.

I watch as the handle on the latch turns slow. The door pushes open a crack. The cold air creeps in. The door creaks, It opens a peep more . . . a peep more.

I stand behind it in the shadows, gripping the fork.

Chapter 28

Two men burst inside. Tight formation. The ginger and the goatee from the pub. I boot the door right back in their faces. The ginger one takes the brunt of the hit, his nose exploding with blood. I grab the other guy by the arm. I throw him across the room, ripping his gun from his hand in the process.

I eject the clip and toss the pistol aside. The ginger bloke staggers around, trying to get a fix on me. Gun in one hand, broken nose in the other.

I move in fast. Twist his shooting arm. Stab the inside of his wrist with the fork. He yells and lets the gun go. There are lots of nerves in the wrist, you see. Motor functions that control the hand. I pull out the fork and throw an elbow. It connects hard and he drops to the deck.

The one with the goatee comes back at me. He has a backup piece inside his leather jacket. Before he can get the safety off, I grab him by the hair. I yank his neck to one side and drive the fork into his head a centimetre behind the ear.

He screams. I twist the fork in deeper. He drops to the

floor, whimpering. I shut the front door and apply the latch.

The guy with the fork in his neck holds the handle, but doesn't dare pull it out. His ginger-haired pal sits with his back against the wall.

I gather their weapons and spill them onto the coffee table. I turn the TV low, pick up a gun and slam in the loose clip. I hold it on the two intruders.

"Don't worry," I say to the guy with the fork in his head. "I'll use my fingers."

I return to my fish and chips. Both my attackers are in agony, bleeding in different ways. I offer them the paper. "Chip?" The pair of them shake their heads. "Suit yourselves," I say, stuffing a piece of battered fish in my mouth. I wolf it down and lick the grease off my fingers. "So, which one of you gentlemen knows where I can find Chris Randall?" I sip on my can of coke. They keep it zipped. "Sorry?" I say, holding a hand to my ear. "I didn't quite catch that."

They refuse to talk. I get up and walk over to the one with the goatee. I turn the fork handle some more.

He screams. *"We don't fucking know!"*

"That's odd," I say. "Sounded like you said you don't know."

I keep twisting.

The guy sobs in pain. "We dunno, please. Please don't—"

I let go of the handle. He doesn't know. I turn to interrogate the ginger guy with the busted up nose. He slips out of the door. Sneaky bastard undid the latch behind my back.

He does a runner, so I return to the sofa and pick up a

chip. The remaining guy sits on the floor, as if waiting for my command.

"Go on then, fuck off," I say. "But whoever you're working for, tell 'em not to bother coming for me. I'm coming for them."

The guy gets to his feet.

"You can keep the fork, I'll keep the guns," I say. "Oh, and close the door behind you. There's a draught."

The guy hurries out of the door. He pulls it closed. I polish off the rest of my chippy tea and relax with a brew on the sofa, satisfied with a good little start to my campaign. They took the bait like I thought. And now I've got myself some guns.

Chapter 29

Eight in the morning. I head out first thing for a brew and a sausage butty. I find an internet café and take a seat at a terminal. The desks are cramped, the computers slow. But the place is clean and modern and they let you make your own brew. Which I like, 'cause most places put in too much milk or too little. Or they tickle it with the teabag and you end up drinking brown water.

I tuck into the sausage butty and open the file Detective Clarke gave me. I look at what they've got. Not much after four to five years. It's like watching highlights from a nil-nil game of footie. Opportunities are few. Whoever they're after, they're no slouches. The bosses remain in the background. And they have a network of bent coppers to call on. Meaning they're always ready in advance when the police carry out a raid on any of their compounds. They move their workers around, too. Run a clean shop. Launder money through a spider's web of companies and off-shore accounts. I mean, you'd need to be that Wolf of Wall Street bloke to figure this stuff out. The likes of Clarke and Morales have no chance.

And that's the problem with coppers these days. Budgets are tight. There's a mountain of red tape. Their foot-soldiers have mortgages, car payments, credit card bills and very flexible loyalties.

Their targets are better funded, organised and equipped. Operating across continents, changing structures faster than the cops can keep up, with blue-chip operational security and boiler-rooms of hackers running counter-intel on Interpol. So this file . . . It may as well be full of dirty bog roll. I close the file and finish my sandwich. I click through to Google. One thing I do know for sure—if Randall is on their payroll, they're a serious outfit. That guy earns a solid crust. Double what I used to charge. The smugglers look as if they're using Ostend to Ramsgate to bypass Calais to Folkestone. Security isn't so tight in the smaller ports. They're also paying or intimidating locals with sailing boats. The journey's a bit longer, but what do the smugglers care? It's smart. It's random. And almost impossible for customs to pick up on. No wonder Clarke helped me escape from that hospital. I'm his only hope of getting anything done. I finish my brew. There's only one place to start here, and that's with the only thing I've got: that I wasn't the only body Randall's goons were trying to cover up in that pit.

* * *

A little known fact about mortuaries: the staff are among the easiest to slip a few quid to.

Probably 'cause no one comes sniffing around, sticking their beaks into their business.

Over the years I've had many a coroner come to the wrong conclusion. Even had bodies 'lost' during the post-mortem. So it's no surprise the assistant in the Croydon Public Mortuary lets me spend a few minutes with the dead.

He pushes his glasses up the bridge of his nose. A pale young chap with a mess of ginger hair and a half-hearted attempt at wearing a tie. He ushers me into a cold, grey room with big white lockers along the back wall. In the middle of the room, there's a body lying on a slab. Dark skin and long brown hair.

The place reeks of strong, sickening chemicals. The lad's white lab-style coat dotted with faded yellow stains.

The sight of the woman is horrific. A large hole cut in her chest. The ribcage pulled apart and the heart missing.

"This is your body," the assistant says.

"Was she beaten up or something?" I ask, walking around the slab, staring at the black and blue marks on her arms and legs.

"The bruises are post-procedural. I guess from handling during transit." The young lad gawps at me funny. "You look almost as bad as them. What happened?"

I ignore the question. Keep circling the slab. "Any idea who she is?"

"Police found her naked, wrapped in plastic in a cement pit," the lad says. "But odds-on she's here illegally."

"Why'd you say that?"

"See the cuts?" he asks, tracing a gloved finger around the hole in the woman's chest. "Precision work. A surgeon's tools . . . She's not the first we've had in like this. Two months ago, we had a young girl missing her eyes."

I shake my head.

"I know," the lad says. "Of course, most times they take a kidney. Stitch them back up and send them on their way. If it's not done right, some of them bleed internally." The assistant looks at the body through sad eyes. "Either way, all roads lead to Rome."

"Do many of 'em arrive in plastic sheets?" I ask.

"They come in all kinds of ways, but this one was the first to be covered in cement . . . Pretty good place to bury a body . . . And to think, me and my girlfriend were thinking of buying off-plan there."

"The same building site?"

"Yeah, supposed to be new apartments going up there. A big glass tower according to the brochure."

"What happened?"

"Oh, planning permission or something. I won't be moving in there now, anyway. Not with—" He motions to the body.

"Yeah, don't blame you," I say.

"What's your interest in all this?" the lad says. "If you don't mind me asking."

"I do mind you asking," I say, slipping him a second twenty. "And I wasn't here."

Chapter 30

I find another internet café not too far from the mortuary. A quick search brings up Taylor Williams. The company has a glossy website with a list of current projects. I notice there's one down the road. It says the place is an office block under construction. I decide to check it out. A tube ride sees me standing outside the place inside twenty minutes. I look up at the bones of the structure. All metal beams and concrete floors.

Workers in yellow vests and hats swarm the site. I notice a couple coming out of a doorway in the black hoardings that extend around the site.

I nip through it, zipping up my jacket. There's an open-air cloak room with spare hats and vests on hooks.

I take a vest and hat. I pick up a clipboard left on a chair.

I walk across the site, to where a scrawny labourer with yellow teeth stands smoking.

"You know what time we knock off here?" I ask him.

"Half four," he says. "You new?"

"Started today."

"Thought I hadn't seen you. What happened to your face, mate?"

"Got jumped outside a boozer."

"Savage bastards."

"So is it all free migrant labour here, or what?"

"Nah mate. It's all unionised. They've gotta do it proper to get these contracts."

"Oh, right."

The guy laughs. "Don't look so gutted."

"No, surprised, that's all."

"Yeah," he says, "they're fucking invading, aren't they?"

I yawn and look around me. "So, is there anything else on offer here, other than work?" The labourer gives me the blanks. I lean in and talk quiet. "You know, like puff or muff? Anything like that?"

He laughs. "I wish, mate. Just work here. Speaking of which."

He tosses his cig and shuffles off into the ground floor of the building. I decide it's a dead end and turn back across the yard in front of the structure. There's a truck pulling in through a main gate, delivering steel girders. As I walk across the front of the cab, I can't help but notice a flash of orange in the windscreen of the cab. The same as the wagon Randall hired me to drive.

It triggers a memory. Something I didn't notice at the time, on account of me wrestling the driver out of the door. But my brain took it in—it's the same bright orange M. The same damn thing.

I wait for the driver to climb down out of the cab. A fat

bastard, he pulls up his jeans and waves at a guy across the yard.

"Here pal," I say. "That air freshener in your windscreen. Where'd you get it?"

"Huh?" he says, glancing into the cab. "Oh, that? You can't buy one. They're company issue."

"They're in every wagon?"

"Yeah, well, unless the driver prefers the smell of his own farts."

"What company do you work for?" I ask.

He taps his fingers against the door. A logo in orange print: *Matheson Haulage*. There's a phone number in small lettering underneath. As the driver walks off towards the back of the trailer, I dial the number of the company on my phone.

A woman answers. I ask her for the address.

Chapter 31

The tube and train take me an hour combined. It's a further twenty minutes on foot before I see the sign for East Thistle Industrial Estate.

The sky is fresh and clear, but the scenery grim. A sprawling old complex of concrete and steel. Trucks, vans and beaten-up cars parked outside faceless warehouses and yards.

The place is a maze. Long roads and avenues that all look the same. Articulated wagons rumbling past me every other minute. I should have stolen a set of wheels, but I'm trying to break the habit. People depend on their cars, after all. You know, to go to work. Pick up the kids. Do their shopping. Probably not fair, swiping their pride and joy from under their noses.

After a while, I find the place. It's fronted by bushes and trees. A wide two-way entrance with a fancy black sign: the same orange logo.

A large security lodge stands to the right with yellow barriers across the entrance.

I approach the security lodge. It's a grey box with a flat

roof and large glass windows. There's only one guard on duty—a stocky black guy with speckled grey stubble.

I linger out of sight behind the sign. Before long, an articulated truck rumbles towards the exit. It stops outside the lodge. I seize the moment and come out of hiding.

I slip into the yard unseen by the guard, the truck between me and the security lodge.

As the truck pulls out of the depot, I slow to a walk, already well past the lodge.

I wear the high vis vest I took from the construction site. And carry a black rucksack, the hard hat tied to one of the straps.

The truck yard is almost empty, but there's a couple of big trailers parked up side by side.

Across the yard is a large orange warehouse next to a three-storey office building. I enter through the warehouse. In fact, it's more than a warehouse. There's a pallet factory deeper into the building. Looks like they make and store 'em. Giant stacks of the things run along the walls to my left and right. And beyond that, a production line manned by guys in ear defenders and safety glasses. They also wear white hard hats and yellow vests like mine.

I walk across the warehouse floor.

I'm approached by a short, pudgy pit bull with a clipboard in hand.

"Oi you," he says.

Shit, busted already.

The guy points to a nearby wall, stickers with safety reminders.

There are two yellow bins beneath the signs. Both full of safety glasses and ear defenders. I slap my forehead as if I forgot. I head straight for the bins. I slip on all the gear, including my hat. I rap my knuckles on the hat and give the guy the thumbs up. Satisfied, he stomps off.

I wander through the warehouse. Not even sure what I'm looking for. But the name of the company is all I've got.

So I pick my way through criss-crossing fork lifts. There's a steel staircase to my left that leads to a mezzanine level. A long line of windows at the top of the stairs.

I walk past the stairs, through the warehouse. I stop to pick up a bag of cement off an open pallet. Heave it over one shoulder.

Gotta look busy. Hides my bruised and battered face, too.

I pass through the pallet factory floor. It's too noisy to strike up a conversation with a worker, so I continue on until I come to a doorway. It's covered by black rubber flaps. It leads into a corridor. The corridor leads to a large garage with truck cabs tilted forward to expose their engines. I ditch the bag of cement and weave through the garage floor. It's noisy and busy. The shrill cry of power drills. The blare of a radio. The smell of oil and grease. Mechanics stand on cabs with their heads buried in engines. I ghost through unseen. Past the entrance where they drive the trucks in, and through another door on the opposite end. It's another corridor, with a series of those rubber flaps at regular intervals. Extractor fans whir overhead. The last rubber divider leads me to a fire exit at the end of the corridor. The door is open. There's a yard outside with a white van with its rear doors wide open. Two guys in check shirts load it up with twenty kilo bags of soil and fertiliser.

I duck out of the way while their backs are turned. Take a sharp left. Yet another face full of doorway flaps and—*Holy shit. I just hit pay dirt.*

Chapter 32

A dingy industrial room sits bare, apart from a pallet of cash and another with kilo packages in a silver foil wrap. A money counter sits on top of a desk against a wall with a chair pushed underneath. I pick up a foil package and dig into it with the key to my flat.

The end of the key comes out dusted in a fine white powder. If it was any good, the stuff would be rockier and yellow in colour.

Yeah, this stuff is cut to high heaven. Looks as if they're packing up and shipping out, too. I wander over to a battered steel door at the back of the room.

As I slide it open, I'm greeted by a dark room with a low ceiling and a herbal whiff strong enough to knock out an elephant.

There's a mini laboratory on the far side and rows of plant life between. The cannabis farm looks as if it's being shut down too, with a pair of guys in lab coats and masks boxing up the plants.

I pull back and shut the door before they notice. I return to the pallets and unzip my rucksack. I throw in a few bags of powder and move onto the cash. The money is shrink-wrapped in clear plastic stacks of hundred-pound notes. There must be five grand in each. And hundreds of stacks on the pallet. I work fast, I chuck a few in the rucksack. I load in another. And pick up one more for the road.

"Who the fuck are you?"

One of the guys from the van stands behind me in the doorway to the room. He's young, Hispanic. A sharp haircut. The shape of a pistol butt beneath the tail of his untucked shirt.

I freeze, cash in hand. "Well this is awkward."

"I said, who are you?" the guy says, removing a pair of mustard work gloves. "What are you doing back here?"

"What does it look like?" I say, dropping the final stack of money inside the rucksack. I leave a hand inside the bag, on the Beretta I stole from the goateed intruder. I take a not-so-wild punt. "I'm one of Randall's guys."

The lad chews on a piece of gum. Scowls at me. "It's not Randall's to take."

And we have a bite.

I take my hand off the gun. I zip up the rucksack and strap it over both shoulders, walking towards the lad. He tenses up. His hand close to his hip.

"Look pal," I say. "I'm just following orders like you."

The guy's eyes narrow. *"You don't know Randall."*

"What, sandy hair? Cocky bastard? Drives a Land Rover? Nah, I don't know him, mate . . . Listen call him if you like."

"Maybe I will," the guy says, hitting a number on his phone.

I hear it ring, the sound echoing off the walls.

As I hear Chris pick up on the other end, I drive a fist into the young guy's face. I catch the phone as he drops it. I cut off the call. The lad rests against the wall on the seat of his pants, sparked out. I copy Chris' number onto my own phone. I drop the young guy's mobile and stomp it to bits.

The fastest way out of this dump is the yard. But the lad's mate is coming the other way, returning to the main building. He catches sight of me. I turn and retrace my steps up the corridor, acting casual.

I glance over a shoulder.

The guy spots his partner unconscious in the room. "Hey, you!" he shouts.

I shrug and carry on walking.

The guy's on a walkie talkie, saying there's been a breach. His weapon off his hip and in his hand. I break into a run, wishing I hadn't loaded the bag up with so much weight. The guy gets a round off as I push through the first rubber divider, wondering why I didn't take his mate's gun.

You sloppy bastard, Charlie.

As I push through the next set of flaps, I hit the brakes, throw myself against the wall to my left. A bullet cuts through the rubber. I hear the kid come running. As he bursts through the divider, I lunge forward and slam him into the wall opposite. I rip the gun from his hand and swipe it across the bridge of his nose.

He's not getting up any time soon, so I move on, through the garage. The mechanics stand gawping. None of 'em say a word. I cut through the cabs, stuffing the gun in the back of my jeans. I pick up the bag of cement and play it cool, strolling away and onto the factory floor.

But it's clear I'm fooling no one. Three more guys stride my way, shoulder to broad shoulder. No safety gear on these blokes. Safety's the last thing on their mind as they block my path out of the factory. One has a hammer. Another a wrench. All three a similar size to me, with beards of different lengths and colours. I stop in my tracks and smile. I hurl the bag of cement at the one to my right. The dumb bastard drops the wrench to catch it. I whip my hat off and strike it across the temple of the middle guy.

I lean away from the swing of the hammer and seize a plank of wood heading for a circular saw on a conveyor belt behind me. I whack the third guy with it and I'm down to one man standing. I swing the plank at him as he charges me. The wood connects with his elbows and splinters in two. The guy barges me back onto the conveyor belt. The left side of my face a centimetre from the spinning saw.

The guy leans his weight on me, trying to push my head into the blade. I raise my knees and push him off with both feet. He runs again. I draw the stolen gun from behind my back and drop him with two fast bullets.

He writhes on the deck. One in the knee. Another in the shoulder.

I take off fast across the warehouse. As a forklift passes by, I hop on the side and put the gun to the driver's head. "Take me to the exit," I say.

He nods, terrified. Puts his foot down, beeping people and traffic out of the way. We break out into the daylight. I jump off and start running, looking around the truck yard for some faster wheels.

But I don't get far. A black Range Rover drives at speed towards the main building. It skids sideways to a stop. Two men in dark clothing leap out. Greying, ex-army haircuts and side arms at the ready. I'm already back-pedalling between those articulated trailers.

I duck low and see the feet of the men running left and right. They're splitting up, taking either end. Shit. They're pros. Private security. None of these factory cowboys.

I back up against the nearest trailer. Gotta think of something. And fast.

Chapter 33

I wait for the two men to jump out on me, either side of the truck. They do. Weapons out. They lower them. I'm not there. Lying on the roof of the left hand trailer, I roll over and swing myself down. I hit the ground running, straight to the Range Rover. I climb inside, my rucksack already off and slung onto the passenger seat.

The engine's running. I shut the driver door and put it in reverse. The two men aren't fooled for long. They sprint into view, unloading rounds as I back up fast. I weave left to right, making myself a harder target. A bullet chips the right side of the bonnet. Another two puncture the windscreen, top and centre. But otherwise, we're golden. I spin the Range Rover and the passenger door swings itself shut.

I speed towards the security barrier. Slam on the brakes. Aim my gun at the guard inside the lodge. He pushes the button. The barrier lifts. I nod in thanks and step on the accelerator, tyres screaming as I belt out onto the road, cutting up a honking truck as I go. I floor the thing all the way out of the industrial estate. Now I've got three guns.

Chapter 34

I drive straight to a used car dealer close to where I've been living. A small forecourt jammed nose to tail with cars of all makes. Some newer than others, but each one at least a few years old. I park the Range Rover down a side street and pick my way through the cars. The office is a white cabin with blue bunting strung across the front. *Frank Samson Autos* is painted in matching blue lettering on the side.

The door is open. The salesman's out quick to meet me with a sweaty handshake and a smile slicker than his hair. He's young and whippet-thin inside a cheap black suit, white shirt and pink tie.

"Hi I'm Frank. See anything you like?" he says. "What kind of motor are you looking for?"

"Something cheap," I say, "but with a bit of speed."

I notice the lad's name tag says *Frank Sampson Jr.* He taps his bottom lip, his fingernails bitten down to stumps. "Let me see," he says, leading me around the forecourt. "There's a Ford Focus."

"Got anything faster?"

He points to a white Impreza with gold rims and a whopping great spoiler. "How about this bad boy?"

"No, I need something low profile."

Frank chews his lip and thinks a moment. He leads me to a pair of silver saloons around the side of the cabin.

"Fancy a Vectra or Mondeo?"

"Ex-fleet?"

"Yeah, but they've only done ninety-thousand."

I spot a maroon Volvo estate. I circle it. A V6 Turbo badge on the rear. I've driven one of these before.

Okay, I nicked one.

It was a good car. Fast. Solid. Reliable. And no one looks twice at a maroon Volvo. It's got a big boot, too.

"The Volvo for sale?" I ask.

"It's only just come in. The old man hasn't priced it up yet. You paying cash?"

"I was thinking more of a swap deal."

"Depends what you're trading in geez. Whether I can shift it. Is it equivalent value?"

"You can tell me," I say, leading Frank off the forecourt and along the side street. We come to the Range Rover.

"You wanna trade *this* for the Volvo?"

"Yep."

"What's wrong with it?" Frank asks, strolling around the back to the driver's side.

"It hasn't got any documentation."

"You mean it's nicked."

"Would that be a problem?" I ask.

I take it by Frank's silence, it's not the first stolen car they've handled.

He rubs a finger on the bonnet. "What's this?"

I take a closer look. It's a large chip in the paintwork. A graze from a stray bullet.

"Big stone hit me on the motorway," I say, popping the locks.

"And these?" he says, pointing to the bullet holes in the windscreen. "More big stones?"

"A glazer'll fix that in five minutes," I say, opening the driver door so Frank can have a nosey inside. I talk to him like *I'm* the salesman. "Look mate, this is a seventy-grand car. Full leather. All the bells and whistles. Brand new too, take a sniff. You'll get at least sixty for it."

"Fifty, tops," Frank says.

"Either way, you're quids in."

Frank stands and stares at the Range Rover, chewing his lip. "I dunno."

"Do I need to speak to the man in charge?" I ask.

Frank straightens up. "My dad? *No.*" He shakes my hand. "I'll take it."

Five minutes later, I'm driving off the forecourt in a maroon Volvo estate with all the beige trimmings. Zero paperwork. And no questions asked.

Frank waves me off, happy with the deal. Not as happy as me. That Range Rover is hotter than a microwaved spud. Probably fitted with a tracker too.

Best to get rid.

I pull into traffic, take out my wallet and slide out

Detective Clarke's business card. I call up his number and talk as I drive. Much as it galls me, it's time to get the pigs involved.

* * *

Detective Clarke waits in a dark-blue Audi A4. He's parked up under a railway bridge on a gravel road. I stop with my driver's door next to his.

We wind down our windows.

Clarke is halfway through a foot-long Subway. He dumps it on his lap and wipes a spot of mayo off his mouth. "I hope this is gonna be worth it."

I grab one of the bundles of stolen cash and hand it over. I don't let him know I've got more.

Clarke takes it, suspicious.

"Courtesy of Matheson Haulage," I say.

"What do you mean?"

"They're part of it. A big part of it." I point at the cash. "There was a hell of a lot more than that. And merchandise, too."

"Got a sample?" Clarke asks.

"Afraid I'm gonna need it. But the money should get you started. Evidence, right?"

"Not exactly," Clarke says.

He stares at the money like Mandy used to look at presents I got her she didn't like.

The soup-maker.

The draught excluder.

The ring with the bloodstain on it.

But that's another story.

"Alright," I say. "It's a foot in the door, at least. They were clearing out when I got there, but there's gotta be a trail. Maybe you can bug their offices. All they know is I nicked it. They don't know I'm helping you out."

Clarke stashes the cash in his glovebox. "What are you gonna do next?"

I smile and step on the accelerator. I pull away, tyres skidding on the gravel. I find Randall's number on my phone and dial. The line rings for what seems like an age.

I'm about to hang up when he answers. "Uh, hello?"

"Chris," I say. "It's your old mate Charlie. How are you doing?"

"Charlie, um, what do you want?"

"I wanna meet. Me and you. No one else."

"And why would I wanna do that?"

"Because I've got some of your drugs. And I doubt you want 'em falling into the wrong hands."

"Whose hands would those be?"

"I dunno, say, the porky pigs?"

"Ah, so that's what the raid was all about? You want a payday."

"You said it yourself. Better than waiting on tables."

"Haven't you stolen enough of our money already?"

"I prefer the word *acquired*."

"And this has got nothing to do with the building site?"

"It wasn't personal, Chris. I stuck my nose in and got what was coming. I shouldn't have opened that trailer."

"I did try and warn you."

"Yeah, but you know what I'm like. Just make sure you come alone."

"I haven't agreed yet."

"Good lad," I say. "I'll text you the time and place."

I hang up on the bastard. Some of these gangs have tracing technology. You can't be too careful. Now all I need to do is find somewhere to meet.

Chapter 35

Derelict tower blocks rose high with hollow windows. According to a sign on the fence surrounding the complex, scheduled for demolition.

Junkies and the homeless loitered in open doorways. There were four towers in total, forming an armed guard against the wind; a square courtyard in the middle.

The exodus of residents had worked in one respect. Even the gangs weren't interested in owning an unprofitable piece of turf.

Waverley Towers was that kind of place. Or at least, Chris Randall thought so. He lit his third cigarette and leaned back against his dark-blue Land Rover. He sniffed the air. Other than burning tobacco, it smelled of something dead and infected.

He couldn't wait to get out of there. Something about the towers—they gave him the creeps.

To make matters worse, Breaker was late. Very late. Chris might have suspected something was off, except he knew the guy wasn't that smart.

If he was, he wouldn't have raided the Matheson operation. Wouldn't have come back at all. On past jobs, he'd caught Breaker talking to thin air on more than one occasion. The guy was clearly nuts.

Chris breathed a heavy, nicotine sigh. How the hell was Breaker even alive? In front of the boss, he'd blamed the two imbeciles he'd left to finish the job. Privately, he blamed himself. He should have felt for a pulse. Checked for a breath. Put a bullet in the man's brain.

Made sure.

Chris shook his head and kicked his heel against a fat Land Rover tyre.

"What's up?" the gruff voice of Jimmy asked in his ear.

"Nothing," Chris said, taking another drag.

"Where is this dickhead?" Jimmy asked.

"Be patient," Chris said. "Stick to your post."

"I think this is bullshit," said Bogdan.

"I don't pay you to think," Chris said.

"You don't pay us at all," Marlon said.

"No, but I do decide who gets what," Chris said. "So shut the fuck up."

Marlon, Jimmy and Bogdan were temps drafted in by his client, at his own recommendation. You didn't always know what you were getting with temporary muscle. But the rotation of staff kept the police from building up a clear who's who. And if a temp got dragged in by the Old Bill, they were even more in the dark than the detectives working the case.

The strategy had paid dividends so far, but jobbing

muscle came at a price. They moaned and groaned all day long. If not about their payment terms, then about the job itself. The hours, the plan, the cold, the boredom, the hunger—they griped about everything.

Chris smoked a fourth and a fifth cigarette. The longer he waited, the more edgy he became. He checked his watch. Called Breaker's number. Straight to voicemail.

"I'm here," Chris said. "Alone like you asked . . . Show up soon or you're fucking dead . . . Again."

"He's not coming," Jimmy said. "Told you he's not coming. Let's go the pub."

"We're not going anywhere," Chris said.

"Hang on a second," Marlon said. "Got a guy on a mountain bike. He's riding past me, heading your way."

"Is it him?" Chris asked.

"Don't know what he looks like, do I?" Marlon said.

"He's a big fucker," Chris said. "Face beaten to shit. You can't miss him."

"Too far away," Marlon said. "Black hoodie and a scarf over his face."

"I see him," said Bogdan. "Rucksack on his back. Could be him. Looks pretty big."

"Okay, get ready," Chris said. "I'll take delivery of the package. Wait for my signal."

Chris turned to see a figure in a black hoodie approaching. Scarf worn like a mask over his face. Gloves on his hands. Black combats and boots completing the look. It was understandable that Breaker would cover his face. He was a wanted man. Though his choice of wheels, he couldn't explain.

As Breaker cut a direct path towards him, Chris ran through the plan in his own mind one more time. Reclaim the merchandise. Pay the money. Let Breaker leave.

Marlon, Bogdan and Jimmy were hiding in the ground floor entrances of the first three buildings. They'd surround him at the right time and gun him down. Chris himself would bring up the rear with his own weapon. Breaker wouldn't stand a chance. And this time he'd put a bullet in the man's skull, personally.

The fact that the guy wanted to meet at all meant he was either desperate or stupid. Whichever it was, he was approaching fast.

Chris tossed the butt of his cigarette and picked up the black rucksack Breaker had requested. He stepped into view, away from the Land Rover and held out a hand. The rider came to a sudden stop, brakes whining. He stared at Chris. Chris stared back. He looked the rider up and down. It wasn't Breaker. The eyes were different. The skin tone darker. And the guy's build nowhere near as broad.

"Who the fuck are you?" Chris asked.

"Got your stuff," the rider said in a young, East End voice.

"Take it slow," Chris said. "You try anything, you're fucking dead."

The rider slipped the rucksack off his back. He held it out for Chris to take. Chris stepped forward. He took the rucksack off the rider. He set his own bag down at his feet and unzipped the other. He looked inside, half expecting a paint bomb to blow up in his face. But the product was there, safe and sound.

Relieved, Chris zipped up the rucksack and set it down at his feet.

"Now the money," the rider said.

Chris picked up the bag with the cash. He held it out for the rider to take.

"Show it me," the rider said.

Chris opened the bag, ignoring the chattering voices in his ear. They wanted to know who it was and when it was time to come out shooting. Chris showed the rider the inside of the bag. He tossed him a stack of notes.

"Sweet," the rider said.

Chris handed the rider the rest of the money. The rider returned the stack of notes to the bag and zipped it closed. He slipped it over both shoulders and swung his bike around. He stood on the pedals and tore away at speed.

"The rider's a kid," Chris said. "Jump him when he gets close."

"What do you want us to do with him?" Jimmy asked.

"We'll find out what he knows," Chris said. "Then we'll get rid of him."

As the rider made his way towards the entrance of the deserted estate, Jimmy ran out and blocked his path. He held a handgun on him while Marlon and Bogdan flanked him from either side.

Chris climbed behind the wheel of his Land Rover. He drove the short distance across the courtyard and came to a stop behind the rider. He got out, weapon drawn by his side. "Hand back the money," he said.

The rider sat with a foot on the ground, gloved knuckles twitching on the handle bars.

Chris raised his gun to the rider's head. "Don't make me ask twice."

Suddenly, Chris heard a clicking of weapons. He looked around the courtyard. Hooded figures appeared in empty window frames. Scarves and bandanas over faces. Guns in hands. From all directions, across several floors, they aimed their weapons square at him and his men. They may have been kids, but there were too many to count in one turn of the head. They had the numbers and the higher ground.

"Better step off me bruv," the rider said.

Chris and his men looked around them one more time. Chris nodded at Jimmy, Marlon and Bogdan. They lowered their weapons as one. Jimmy stepped aside.

The rider pedalled away with an insult under his breath.

Chris looked up and around. The tower block windows empty. The hooded figures gone.

Marlon, a tall Jamaican man with a dress sense from the 70s, flapped his arms. "What do we do now?"

"We've still got the stuff," Chris said. "The boss'll have to do without his money."

"You wanna drive around? Look for this Cobb fella?" Jimmy asked. "He can't be far off."

"Nah," Chris said. "Knowing him, he'll be on his way out of town already." Chris took a last look around the abandoned towers and waved the men into the Land Rover. "Smart, Charlie. Smart."

Chapter 36

I watch Randall smoke another cigarette. He talks to thin air. A sure sign he's brought help.

I decide it's time. I take out my mobile and text Aziz, the tall kid closest to my size.

From the eighth floor of the southern tower block, I've got the perfect view. I zoom in with the long lens camera bought with the proceeds of the Matheson raid. The southern tower stands at the far end of the estate, facing the entrance. I see Aziz appear on his bike. Hood pulled up and scarf over his face like I told him.

I lean with my elbows on a dusty kitchen worktop, camera lined up through a jagged hole in a broken glass window. It smells like a dead rat in here, but better than the lower floors. The squatters and junkies don't tend to make it this high.

I see Randall pick up the rucksack I told him to bring the cash in. Aziz makes a beeline for his Land Rover. Randall steps out and Aziz skids to a stop.

I zoom in closer and adjust the focus. There's a brief standoff.

Aziz takes the rucksack I gave him off his shoulders. He hands it over. Randall opens it slow, like it's a bomb set to go off. He checks out the contents: the kilo packs of cocaine I stole.

Randall takes one out and weighs it in his hand. He seems satisfied. He opens his own bag and tosses Aziz a stack of notes. Shows him the rest of the money. Zips it up and hands it over.

Aziz straps on the bag and pedals out of there. Randall's lips move. I take my head away from the camera to see the bigger picture. I see three tiny figures appear from the ground floor level of the other buildings. I get back behind the camera and zoom in and out, trying to focus.

I get a good look at all three guys. A real mixed bag of nuts. There's a black guy in flares, mint turtle neck and a long brown leather jacket. A bloke with a bald patch on top in a blue tracksuit. Another with a modern side-parted haircut that's too young for him. He wears a black bomber jacket like mine.

They stop Aziz on the way out. Randall, the lazy shit, gets in his Land Rover and drives the short distance across the courtyard. He climbs out with a weapon of his own.

I'm already on my phone. "Now," I tell Mabs, the gang leader.

To his credit, Aziz doesn't panic. I told him this'd happen and he plays his part to a tee.

As Randall puts his gun to Aziz's head, the empty windows of the towers flood with kids from the block where I've been living. Randall and his goons take a look around. They think better of it.

After a long, tense pause, they lower their weapons. The one with the flash haircut steps aside. Aziz rides out of there with the money. Randall and the goons look around again. The kids are already gone from the windows, happy with their haul of cash.

I take a few rapid-fire photos of Randall and his helpers. I take a snap of the Land Rover plate, too.

I pull away from the window and detach the zoom lens from the camera. I pack it away fast in the small black case it came in and make my way out. There's a rear entrance out of the tower where the fence has been torn out of the ground. It leads across a bump of grass onto a side street where I left the Volvo. I climb in and start the engine.

I spot the Land Rover swing by on the main road, stopping at a set of lights. I pull away from the kerb and drive fast to the end of the street. I turn right, a couple of cars between me and the Land Rover.

The lights change and we move.

It's a busy two-lane road, ideal for tailing. I get to within a car of Randall's Land Rover and sit there. I follow them to a row of shops. I park a few bays down. The hired help get out of the Land Rover with the rucksack. They head into a laundrette. Unless they all wash their underpants together, I'd bet any money it's a mafia front.

But it'll have to wait. Randall pulls out into the road again and continues on his way.

I leave it a few seconds before I ease into traffic behind him. We come to a large, four-way junction. It's a long wait as each filter lane takes its turn.

Our light is still on red when the Land Rover sets off. It cuts across the junction in a pause between cars.

Meantime, I'm stuck behind a red Astra hatchback. The bastard's getting away. I'm gonna lose him.

Come on you piece of shit, turn green.

Chapter 37

Finally, the light turns. The two cars in front take an age to move, but all I need is a few inches. I pull out and around, wishing I'd gone for the Impreza.

I rag the Volvo up to its limit in each gear, fast-changing to gain some ground. Randall is off and flying along an empty stretch of dual carriageway road. But I make up some of the distance thanks to the turbo engine of the car.

The bastard must have caught on when he dropped off his goons. He pulls a sharp right into a residential neighbourhood. I slam on late and screech into the same road.

Randall's Land Rover is a hundred metres ahead. I'm gaining on every straight, so it's no surprise he takes a sharp left, trying to lose me.

Neither car is built for cornering. The Volvo feels like a boat as I nurse it into a tight avenue lined by small brown council houses and messy lawns.

We turn again, into a longer, wider street. I wind down the window and lean out. Wheel in my left hand. Gun in my right.

I aim for the tyres, but the streets around here are uneven and full of holes. The Volvo bounces and rattles. I only succeed in ruining the Land Rover's paintwork.

But this might be my lucky day.

The road leads into a close. A dead end. Randall brakes and swings the Land Rover round in a big circle. I emergency stop and find reverse.

Randall comes the other way to my right. I step on the accelerator and back it up alongside him.

We ram into each other, taking turns, trying to run each other off the road.

The Land Rover eases past, into the lead. I spin the wheel all the way to the right. The Volvo flips around and I fast-change into third. I give it beans and chase Randall all the way back where we came from.

As we fly towards the T-junction at the end of the road, a large white bin truck pops out of a side street. Randall can't brake fast enough. The nose of the 4x4 slams into the side of the truck. It's a heavy hit. Randall's front end all shot to shit.

I slow and mount the kerb to the left of the road.

As Randall spills out of the driver's seat, he lets off a round. A wild shot that misses completely.

Randall flies past me into a narrow side alley. I'm out of the Volvo, giving chase on foot.

I've got the longer stride. Randall is the lighter and nimbler.

Neither of us are Usain Bolt, but we run full blast along the alley, out across another street.

A young mum pushes a pram across our path. Randall barges her to the ground. I hurdle over the pram and stay on his tail. I tuck my gun away inside my jacket.

I want him alive.

He spots a chance to lose me. A hard right through a gap in a wooden fence. I follow him into a back garden. He tumbles over a hedge. I jump and tumble after him, into another back lawn littered with kids' toys.

I step on a squeaky rubber dog as I run. Randall tips over a green plastic slide. I trip over the damn thing and lose time. As I get up, I see Randall's feet scrambling over a high fence.

Now, if I was him, I'd use the time wisely. I'd crouch down on the other side, ready with my gun.

So, rather than climb over the fence, I run straight at it. I smash through the damn thing and sure enough, he's waiting for me on the other side.

He hesitates in surprise. I snatch his gun with one hand and deliver a knock-out punch with the other. He lies prone on the grass. I put his weapon on safety and zip it up in a side pocket on my bomber jacket.

"Oi, what the fuck are you playing at?" A hairy gorilla in a stained white vest comes out of a back door to the house. "What've you done to my fence?" I try to ignore the guy. He puts a hand on my shoulder. "Oi, dickhead, I'm talking to you."

I put a hand on his throat and squeeze. "Sorry mate, you were saying?"

His head turns purple. His eyes bulge out like soft-boiled eggs.

I let him go. He's got the point. I take a few twenties from my wallet and throw 'em at him. "For the fence," I say.

He splutters and staggers back into the house with his money.

Randall lies sprawled on the patchy green lawn, covered in splintered wooden panels. He sports a nasty bruise around his eye, out for the count and going nowhere in a hurry.

And thank Christ, too. I'm bloody knackered.

Chapter 38

I sit on an upturned blue beer crate, wearing a pair of white latex gloves. I doodle in black pen on a small notepad: a giant rabbit fighting a horse.

Randall murmurs. Starts to come around. The black eye I gave him swallowing an entire socket.

I had to give the guy a few sedatives. Forced 'em down him the first time he woke up.

Lucky for me, he had a bunch of them in his bottom kitchen drawer. One of those designer kitchens with the big fancy mixer taps and black marble tops. A nice place he's got. But we're here in the garage. Me on the crate. Him strung up by the neck by a length of yellow electrical wire.

I tied the wire to one of three steel beams that run sideways under the ceiling. Each beam has a line of holes drilled in for hanging hooks and whatever else. Very handy for suspending a man from the ceiling.

Randall picks his head up. The wire in a noose around his neck. Wrists taped around his back. Feet arranged on a side table I found in his hallway. I've also fixed a broom between his arse and the floor to keep him upright.

He starts awake and struggles for balance. The broom falls to the floor. I react, thinking he's gonna slip off the table, but he rights himself. Finds his feet. I return to the crate. Keep doodling while he gets his bearings.

Doesn't take long for him to work out his predicament.

His first words: "How did you know where I lived?"

He's asking because the address on his driving licence is a fake.

"Dry cleaning receipt in your pocket," I say, finishing the drawing. "Nice gaff. No wife or kids?"

I already know the answer. I checked for photos when I first came in the house. I just want to get his brain working again. I need the bastard lucid.

A wry smile breaks on his face. "Who needs a wife when you've got Tinder? Know what I'm saying?"

"Not really. I still don't know what that Tinder thing is," I say, resting my pen on the pad, pulling my handgun from my shoulder holster.

I slide the chamber. It's clean. Check the clip. I've got enough.

"So what do you want, Charlie?"

"You know the drill," I say.

"What's that?"

"Dunno whether you've noticed, Chris, but time isn't on your side."

Randall gazes at the tips of his shoes.

"Give me a name," I say.

"Then what? You shoot me anyway?"

I return my gun to my holster. Hold out both hands. "You have my word." Randall doesn't make a peep. "Come on, Chris. Who's behind this?"

"Ain't no one behind it," Randall says. "It's all on me. All of it."

I look around me. Stand up off the crate. "No offence pal . . . Nice as this place is, you don't get many bosses living in a three-bed semi."

Randall shuffles from foot to foot. "What can I say? I'm settled."

I stretch and yawn. Shake my head. Pick up an axe I left resting blade-down against the wall. "What's this for?" I ask, weighing it in my hands. "Wood burning stove?"

"Chiminea," Randall says, grimacing in pain. Flexing his wrists inside the tape. "The birds love it."

"You sly bastard," I say with a smile. "Must be great to have a silver tongue like yours. Being able to talk your way in or out of anything." I wrap both hands around the axe handle. "Now would be a good time to start using it."

Randall huffs. "Whatever you think you can do to me, it's nothing compared to what they will."

"Oh, I don't know about that."

I swing the axe and chop the left rear leg off the table.

The table rocks, but holds.

Randall panics, but keeps his feet.

The wire creaks as he steadies himself, the table down to three legs.

"You ever see a man hang by the neck?" I ask, air-swinging

the axe. "Most people top 'emselves thinking it'll be quick . . . It's not."

Randall looks close to cracking. "Alright Charlie. How much?"

"How much of what?"

"Of whatever it is you want. Money? Drugs? A stake in the game?"

I laugh. "I don't want your money, mate. You haven't got enough anyway."

"I didn't mean from me, dickhead. I can get it you from . . ."

"From who? Come on, you almost said it then."

Randall shakes his head. "You're a lot of things. But this ain't you, Charlie."

I sigh and swing the axe. Another leg goes. The front right. A clean strike.

The noose catches tighter around Randall's neck. He splutters. Straightens up. The guy's got good balance. I'll give him that.

"Three strikes and you're out pal," I say, parking my behind on the crate. I rest the axe on my lap and pick up my notepad and pen. "Come on, names and addresses."

Randall breathes fast and shallow. Gets angry. Snot spitting out of a nostril. *"Go to fuck."*

I put down the notepad and pen. Stand up and stretch. "Maybe I'm losing my touch," I say, cracking my neck side to side. I line the axe blade up with the nearest remaining table leg. I bring it back and let it swing.

"Prince!"

I stop the axe an inch short of the leg.

Randall eyes the blade. His voice wobbles. "Eddie Prince. That's the name you're after."

I withdraw the axe and relax my grip. *"Eddie Prince?"*

"Just said it, didn't I?"

"You're telling me that dickhead's the brains behind a Europe-wide firm? Pull the other one."

"That's the only name I've got," Randall says. "I take my orders from him. That's as far up as I go. And I don't wanna go any further, either."

I rest the axe against the wall. "Where does he live?"

"I dunno."

"Don't bullshit me."

"The guy may be a prize arsehole, but he's not stupid. He rinses some of his cash through a laundrette. I meet him in there."

"The place you dropped your cronies off?"

"Supersuds, yeah. Ask for Dave. He'll know."

I pick up my notepad and pen. I rest them on the crate. "Didn't need these after all."

Randall breathes a sigh of relief. "I've given you the name. Now cut me down, yeah?"

I stand, arms folded. "Don't remember that being part of the deal."

"You said you weren't gonna kill me."

"I'm not," I say, walking around the back of Randall. He's got a nice red tool bench with see-through drawers underneath. I pull out a drawer and take out a set of wire cutters with orange rubber grips. "These should do the trick," I say walking around the front of him. I reach up and slip them in the left breast pocket of his blue denim shirt.

"What the—Charlie what are you doing?"

I reach inside his trouser pocket and grab his mobile. I transfer it to the right breast pocket of his shirt.

"Charlie, what the fuck—"

There's panic in his eyes. He cottons on quick.

I fix him with a smile. "Figure your way out of this one, Chris."

I walk out of the door into the house.

Randall rocks on the table. It groans under his weight. *"Charlie! Charlie! Charlie you fucking—"*

I close the door behind me, muffling his cries. I walk through the house. The smell of new carpet in the air. I return to the kitchen and open a top drawer. I take a fork out of a cutlery tidy. Premium stainless steel. Nice. I slip it inside a jacket pocket. "There," I say to myself. "Now we're even."

Chapter 39

Amira lingered under the shower, a jet of hot water massaging her aching shoulders.

After changing into a white robe and slippers, she stepped out into the bedroom. She expected to see her pile of dirty clothes on the carpet by the bed.

They were gone.

Someone had taken them while she was in the bathroom. In their place, they'd left a set of white linen pyjamas, folded on the bed.

The bed itself had been made during her shower.

Made from the night before, where she'd slept for twelve hours straight. She'd woken up to a continental breakfast, left on a bedside table. The tray with leftover fruit, meat, bread and cheese was gone too. The curtains thrown open, letting the sunlight in.

Pyjamas seemed a deliberate choice, bearing in mind it was afternoon. After all, where would Amira go without shoes or outdoor clothes?

She changed into them anyway: comfortable and airy against her skin.

Amira tied the thick, Egyptian cotton robe around her waist. She pushed her feet into her soft slippers and walked around the room. She looked out of each window and counted six floors to ground level. Her room looked out over a pristine courtyard: outdoor furniture and royal-blue gazebos. It was a nice day.

She crept towards the door. She held her breath and put an eye to the spy hole. She expected to see a guard on the other side of the door.

She didn't. So she tried the brass door handle.

Surely it would be locked.

It wasn't.

Amira eased the door open. The room was at the end of a plush corridor, lit with soft white ceiling lights. She slipped out through the door and eased it closed. She hurried along the corridor and found a pair of elevators a little further down.

She jabbed on a button. The elevator to her right was heading up. She looked both ways as the numbers on the digital display rolled over from three, four, five... The doors opened with a bright ping. The elevator was empty. She jumped inside and selected the ground floor.

The doors seemed to take an age to close.

Amira tugged at a strand of hair, wet and straggled from the shower.

She wasn't even sure what the plan was when she reached the hotel lobby. Raise the alarm with the hotel staff? Head straight for the main entrance and make her escape?

She decided that getting clear of the hotel was best. No

delays. She would figure the rest out in due course.

The elevator cruised down to the ground floor. The doors opened and she exited into the lobby.

The open backs of her slippers flapped against a polished marble floor. She saw the exit ahead. An automated, revolving glass door. Sunlight flooding in. She noticed a female receptionist behind the main desk, but felt she couldn't trust her. What if the hotel staff were in on it?

No, head for the exit. Get clear of the hotel. Stick to the plan.

Halfway across the lobby, a large man with a greased black pony tail stepped into her path, as if he'd been waiting for her.

He seized Amira by the arm.

Amira looked up at him. Across to the woman on reception. The woman noticed, but disappeared through a side door, as if instructed.

"I told Tony to give you a little space," a voice said from behind a newspaper. It came from a man to her immediate right, reclining in a coffee-coloured armchair. He lowered the newspaper and folded it in two. It was Pavel. "Didn't want you thinking you were here against your will."

"Then I'm free to leave?"

"I think it's best if you stay," Pavel said, throwing out his arms. "A good place to relax awhile, no?" He motioned for Tony to let go of Amira's arm.

Tony let go.

"Did you sleep well?" Pavel asked, rising out of his chair.

Amira pinched her robe tight to her neck. "Where are my clothes?"

"I hope you don't mind," Pavel said. "I had them thrown away."

"Then what am I supposed to wear?"

"I'll have something sent up to you." Pavel checked his phone. "I've got to go. In the meantime, relax and enjoy the room. Tony and the hotel staff will take care of you."

Pavel turned to leave.

"What am I doing here?" Amira yelled after him.

Pavel spoke over his shoulder. "I'll see you later, Amira."

They knew her name. How did they know? Her passport? It was the only way. Which meant Pavel was one of the gang that had abducted her and the others off the coach. From the cut of his suit and the five-star surroundings, Amira assumed he must have been some kind of boss. Someone with access to money. And lots of it.

Tony pointed to the elevators. Amira turned and walked towards them.

Chapter 40

Supersuds is like any other laundrette. Wall-to-wall washing machines and top-loading dryers. Big, old coin-operated things. Boxes of cheap washing powder and baskets of clothes left on top. There's an empty counter at the far end. A rack of dry-cleaned items hung up in white covers. And two rows of red plastic chairs, back to back.

It's dark outside by the time I enter. An obese black woman in a purple velour tracksuit sits alone inside. She has short, platinum blonde hair and a bored expression. She does the crossword on the back of a newspaper.

I peel off my bomber jacket and pull my t-shirt off over my head.

The woman pretends not to look. Raises an eyebrow. Huffs to herself.

I kick off my boots and socks. I unbuckle my jeans and step out of the legs.

Damn, I wore the Donald Duck boxers.

I bundle my dirty clothes together on a chair—the t-shirt

sweaty from the foot race with Randall. My jeans with grass stains on the knees.

I take a note from my wallet and pad barefoot to the front counter. I push a buzzer on the top.

It buzzes.

A tiny shrivelled woman trudges out in blue overalls. Hair pulled back and skin like a used carrier bag.

"Is Dave around?" I ask.

She talks in a harsh cockney accent. "Who wants to know?"

"Just shout him, will you?"

"Daaaaaave!" she shouts at the top of her lungs. *"Someone here asking for yer!"*

"Who is it?" Dave yells back from round the corner.

"How the hell should I know?"

I hear the man sigh. He waddles out, pulling his grey joggers up off his arse. He has a chocolate bar in hand. A mouthful he's working on. Greasy black hair, a beard and crumbs all down the front of an AC/DC t-shirt. He looks me up and down. "What have you come as?"

"Are you Dave?"

"What's it to you?"

Yeah, it's Dave.

I lean over the counter and beckon him forward. "I've got something to tell you."

The thick bastard comes in close. I grab him by the neck and slam his forehead into the countertop. The tiny woman shits herself and disappears into the back.

"I wanna know where I can find Eddie Prince."

Dave bleeds from both nostrils. He leaves a chocolate print on the chipped white counter top. *"Who?"* he says in a daze.

I grab his head again, ready to slam him the second time. *"Okay, okay!"* he says. "*Jesus!*"

He mops the blood from his nose with a tissue.

I look at the sheen on my hand, from the grease in his hair. I wipe it off on the counter.

"He lives in some big place in Weybridge,"

"Where's that?"

"Posh part of Surrey."

"Got an address?"

"Uh, we might have it from his dry cleaning." Dave turns and yells into the back room.

"Doreen!"

"What?"

"Look on the computer. Find Mr Prince's address!"

"What for?"

"Just do it!"

Doreen complains bitterly to herself in the back. Dave looks at me. I look at Dave.

"You got the address yet?" he yells over his shoulder.

"I can't find it!"

Dave rolls his eyes and stuffs more of the chocolate bar in his face, as if he's trying to eat the wrapper, too. He waddles off into the back. He reappears soon after with a scrap of paper and an address written in pencil. He pushes it across the counter. A shifty look in his eye.

I glance at the address. *Halewood Castle, 10 Balmoral*

Way. Sounds pretentious. I tuck the slip of paper inside my wallet. I pull out a note. "Got change for a twenty?"

"You've gotta buy something," Dave says.

I look to my left. There's a big jar stuffed with fruit lollipops. A quid each. Daylight robbery. I snatch two from the jar and hand over the twenty.

Dave snorts and rings the till open. Hands me a ten and eight pound coins. I take the lollies and the change. I shove my clothes into the nearest washing machine and pour in the lumpy dregs of an open box of powder. I set it on the quickest programme.

I plonk myself down on the nearest chair, down the row from the woman in the purple tracksuit. She looks up at me. Pulls a face like a constipated duck.

"What?" I say.

"Just my luck," she says. "A guy strips off in the laundrette and it's you."

I suck in my belly and sneer at her. She goes back to her crossword. I tear the wrapper off the first lolly and stick it in my mouth.

Blackcurrant. My favourite.

* * *

It's warm in the laundrette. The churn of machines hypnotic.

We're sitting there for twenty minutes. I'm onto my second lolly: lemon and lime. They're bloody good.

The woman in the purple tracksuit asks me a question. "What's the capital of Peru?"

I turn and look at her. "Eh?"

"Fourteen across, four letters," she says, waiting for an answer.

"How should I know?"

"Ooh," she says shaking her head, "excuse me for breathing."

"You're excused," I say, turning my attention back to the drum of the machine in front of me.

"It's Lima," Cassie says. She sits on the chair to my left.

"What is?" I say.

"The capital of Peru," says Cass, sucking on a lolly of her own.

"Who are you talking to?" the crossword woman asks me.

"None of your business," I say. "But the answer's Lima."

The woman counts the squares on her puzzle. "Huh, it fits," she says, writing it out on the paper.

Cassie shakes her head at my boxer shorts.

"Hey, you loved Donald Duck when you were little."

"So embarrassing," she says.

The woman with the crossword clears her throat. "Whatever imaginary elf you're talking to, ask 'em if they know what a three letter word for annoying is."

I turn to ask Cassie. She's vanished again. If I get clear of this latest mess, I really should call her. Make sure that Sam character's not getting her into trouble.

"Well?" the woman asks me.

"Well what?"

"Three letter word for annoying."

"I dunno, but I'm guessing it starts with *u*."

The woman sneers and moves onto the next clue.

I turn to her and remove the lolly from my mouth. "What's the point in doing the damn thing if you don't know the answers?"

The woman mutters to herself. My washing machine cycle ends. I get up and open the door. I transfer my clothes to a nearby dryer. It swallows another quid. I shut the heavy steel door and it clanks into life.

I hear the front door open. Three men walk in.

Jimmy, Bogdan and Marlon from this afternoon. I shoot a look at Dave. He slides a steel door shut behind the counter.

Damn you, Dave, you double-crossing shit.

Chapter 41

Clarke and Morales climbed out of the Audi into the yellow glow of suburban streetlight. They ducked under the police tape cordoning off the house and showed their badges to the CSO. His name was Waters, a stocky, mixed-race man Clarke had met in passing.

"You guys NCA?" Waters asked.

"Uh-huh," Morales said.

"We've got your man inside," Waters said, leading them in through the front of the house. He showed them to an open door: a private garage inside.

Forensics officers combed the scene. They dusted the house for prints, the chatter of a camera shutter in the background.

Clarke stepped inside the garage, his breath fogging the air. He took an A4 print and held it up alongside the figure hanging from a beam in the roof. He compared the picture to the body.

"This the guy?" Waters asked.

"This is the guy," Clarke said.

"I'll give you a few minutes," Waters said, leaving the garage. "I hate the sight of a hanging body."

"You know guv," Morales said, "you still haven't told me how you got that photo."

"I told you," Clarke said. "It showed up in the mail."

"No, I mean the *real* how."

"So suspicious, Morales," Clarke said, stepping around Chris Randall's body. His feet swung loose below him. A wire cut deep into his throat. Randall's face was pale, drained of blood.

A small oak table lay on its side. Only two legs remaining. The others in splinters on the floor.

Morales pointed to an axe, propped up in the corner. An upturned beer crate nearby, with a notepad and pen on top.

Clarke nodded. The detectives snapped on a pair of gloves each.

Morales picked up the notepad. She tilted her head. "What the hell—?"

"What is it?" Clarke asked.

"You tell me," Morales asked, showing him a black ink drawing on the pad.

"Looks like a kangaroo shagging a camel."

Morales shook her head and returned the pad to the crate.

Clarke lifted a mobile phone from Randall's pocket. "Looks like the killer has a sense of humour."

"Looks like revenge to me," Morales said. "You think it could be Cobb?"

"Why do you say that?" Clarke asked.

"Randall's connected to Matheson Haulage, right?"

"I'm starting to think so."

"Then who's the one guy we know who might have a score to settle?"

Clarke returned the phone to Randall's pocket. "I don't know," he said. "I reckon Cobb will be long gone by now. He's a fugitive, remember?"

Waters reappeared. "So, cracked it yet?" he asked.

"The phone in Randall's pocket," Clarke said. "We'll need access to it."

"I'll get someone on it," Waters said, following them out of the garage. "I'll call you if we find anything. The guy didn't leave any prints."

"I'm not surprised," Clarke said. "Whoever did this is a pro. Probably a hired hit . . . Have the phone sent to me when you're done, will you?"

"Will do mate," said Waters.

Clarke exited the house and strode down the driveway, rolling off his latex gloves and tossing them on the lawn.

"I know it's not my place to ask," Morales said, trailing behind, "but there's something you're not telling me. What is it?"

As the detectives returned to their car, Clarke opened the driver-side door. He paused and looked at Morales across the roof of the saloon, streetlight reflecting in the paintwork. "You're right Morales. It's not your place."

Clarke slipped inside the car. Morales huffed in frustration and climbed in.

Chapter 42

The three amigos split up as they enter. Bogdan saunters to the counter. Marlon leans against a dryer on the far side of the laundrette.

Jimmy approaches the woman on the chairs. He puts a hand on her shoulder. "Place is closing sweetheart. Time to leave."

"It's open until ten-thirty," she says, checking her watch.

Jimmy hauls her up by the elbow, her newspaper and pen in hand. I see her catch a glimpse of his piece inside his jacket. Doesn't stop her arguing.

"But I've got a load in the machine," she says, as she's marched towards the door.

"Come back in ten minutes," Jimmy says, bundling her onto the street. He slams the door shut and applies a bolt at the top and bottom.

I stand with my back to the machines, sucking my lolly.

Jimmy strolls over. "What's this?" he says, looking me up and down. "Woofter hour?"

"Heard you were an arsehole short," I say.

"You the joker who ripped off the Matheson depot?" Jimmy asks.

I eyeball the guy and both of his cronies. I keep my mouth shut.

"What do you want with Eddie Prince?" he continues.

I crunch my way through what's left of the lolly. Loud.

"No one tell you it's rude to eat with your gob open?" Jimmy says, drawing his gun from a shoulder holster.

I crunch even louder. Slower.

Jimmy holds his weapon by his side. He's left-handed. I make a mental note. He waves the barrel at me. "Hands like you're getting a blowjob," he says. "No silly moves."

I finish the lolly. Toss the stick aside. Put my hands behind my head and walk forward a couple of paces.

Bogdan and Marlon close in on me.

I was stupid. Should've got out of this dump. Now I'm stuck here, unarmed and dressed like a total prick.

"Any of you losers married?" I ask. They shake their heads. "Kids?"

Marlon raises a hand. "I've got a boy."

"Ah shit," I say. "Well, I'll *try* not to kill you."

The three men burst out laughing.

"You hear that lads? Donald Duck here is gonna set us straight." Jimmy shakes his head and sighs. "Okay fancy pants, let's take a walk."

Again, we go back to my earlier points of a) space and b) overconfidence.

a) There's a natural tendency for people to crowd around the source of the threat. Remember the two goons in the car?

They get in close, thinking it gives 'em more control. Nope, it only does the opposite.

b) They see an unarmed, battered and bruised mess in his emergency boxers and they relax a little too much.

Bogdan is a classic example. He's lurking on my left shoulder. His weapon is drawn. And he's still laughing when I reach behind and direct his gun towards Marlon.

Bogdan's first instinct is to pull the trigger. An idiot move because it's goodnight Marlon. The guy collapses without getting a shot off in return.

The gun is out of Bogdan's hands before he knows what's happening. But Jimmy's more alert. Next thing, we're in a tangle, both of us trying to get a shot at the other.

Bogdan's back in the game, too. He gets me in a headlock. The three of us collapse to the floor in a heap. I'm on top of Jimmy with Bogdan on my back.

I slam Jimmy's hand against the hard yellow tiles of the laundrette floor. His pistol slides away. My attempt to shoot him in the face fails when Bogdan wrestles me for control.

He ejects the clip from the weapon as Jimmy punches me in the face. I thump Jimmy back, but Bogdan forces the gun from my other hand. I stand up with Bogdan on my back, his forearm crushing my throat

I reverse fast and slam him into a washing machine. He cries out and falls off.

Jimmy scrambles for the gun with the clip still in it. I dive on top of him and punch him hard in the back.

Bogdan rugby-tackles me off him.

As we tumble, I elbow him in the jaw. I grab him by the

neck and slam his head into a washing machine door.

There's a sickening crack. Blood splattered on the glass. I do him again. This time the glass gives way as I drive his head right through, into a load that keeps on churning.

Bogdan's body slumps limp. His head bumping and bashing inside the drum.

Blood, bone and soapy water flood the floor.

I turn to see Jimmy picking himself up. A hand on his spine. I walk across the floor towards Marlon. He's closest. His gun still in his cold, dead hand.

But I get cocky myself. I slip on the soapy water spreading fast over the floor. I land heavy on my back, catching my head on the lip of a plastic chair.

I lie between a line of tumble dryers and the row of seats. The back of my skull rages. I go to get up. Jimmy snatches the weapon from Marlon's hand. He pushes me back down. His weight on my chest. The gun in my face.

"Right, you fucker," he says. "Time to—"

I slam a steel dryer door into Jimmy's face. He sways dizzy, his weight still on me. The gun held by his side, out of reach.

I stretch out a hand and grab my belt off the chairs. I loop it around his neck and pull it tight.

I use the belt to lever him off me. Then I get behind him and pull like I'm trying to stop a galloping horse. He lets off a round over his shoulder, trying to shoot me in the face.

He misses. The gun slips out of his hand, covered in soapsuds.

I hold on tight until his tongue hangs loose out of his

mouth. I let him drop, get to my feet and tiptoe through the water.

I open the door to the dryer my clothes are in. They're nice and toasty.

The crossword woman's load finishes too. I root inside her dryer and find a towel.

She's got a husband by the looks of it. A big fella. I dry myself off with the towel and change into a pair of his baggy white boxers. I pull on my own clothes and boots. I swing my bomber jacket on as the steel door to the back office slides open. Dave pops his head out. Nerves replaced by shock.

"Better get a mop, Dave," I say, fixing my belt and loading my pockets with wallet and keys. I fold up my Donald Ducks and stuff 'em in a jacket pocket.

Don't wanna leave any evidence. And besides, they were a present from my nan.

I unbolt the door to the laundrette and hit the streets. That nice feeling of a set of clean clothes, warm out of the dryer.

If Eddie Prince didn't know I was coming for him before, he sure does now.

Chapter 43

A knock on the door. The door opened a foot. Three boxes slid inside. Each on top of the other.

The disturbance woke Amira from an afternoon snooze. She slipped out of bed and walked barefoot in her pyjamas across the soft carpet. She knelt down and picked up the boxes.

All three were of different shapes, sizes and weights. Each made of the same black laminated cardboard, tied with pink ribbon.

She carried them to a nearby writing desk and loosened the ribbons. She found the top box filled with a range of cosmetics, still in their wrappers.

Amira put it to one side. The second box contained a pair of black designer high-heeled shoes in her size.

The third and final box was flat and wide. Amira opened the lid to reveal a folded dress wrapped in crepe paper.

A small, square note lay on top: *Dinner, 7:00PM*

Amira pulled the dress from the box.

It was olive green. Silk and backless with straps around

the neckline. Amira checked the label. Expensive.

She let the dress fall loose in her hands and held it against her body in a full-length mirror. It ended just above her knees and from what she could tell, it would fit.

The dress, like the shoes and cosmetics, was beyond anything she could have afforded on her teacher's salary at home. And no doubt, it was paid for in blood.

The question was—was she willing to wear it?

* * *

The Mercia Hotel Restaurant was lit low in a red and black colour scheme. Light piano music tinkled in the background. A smattering of diners sat across from one another, engaged in quiet conversation.

Tony had escorted her to the restaurant. Amira felt sure he would be there to escort her back to the room.

Now an efficient blonde maître d' led her across the spacious restaurant floor.

Pavel sat at a table for two. He wore a tailored black suit and matching tie. He rose to his feet as she approached, looking her up and down. "Wow," he said.

The maître d' pulled out a chair across from Pavel. Amira lingered on her feet.

"Please, sit," Pavel said.

As Amira took her seat, the maître d' handed her a leather-bound menu.

Pavel returned to his seat. "It's okay," he said, "She'll have what I'm having."

"Certainly, sir," the maître d' said, taking the menu off

Amira. She glided clear of the table.

"Well," Pavel said, pouring Amira a glass of white wine. "You look sensational... I *knew* you had potential. Something of a talent of mine."

Amira picked up the glass. She didn't usually drink, but these were extenuating circumstances.

"So, tell me about yourself, Amira."

"Tell you what?"

"Your English is excellent. I can tell you're educated. University? Post-graduate?"

Amira said nothing.

Pavel sipped on his wine. "Mm, post-graduate."

A waiter appeared with two starter plates in hand. "Confit of duck," he said, resting the plates in front of Pavel and Amira.

"Sorry, I forgot to ask," Pavel said, arranging a napkin on his lap. "Do you eat meat?"

Amira nodded.

"Then *tuck in*, as the British say."

Amira picked up a polished fork. Heavy. Silver. She stabbed a small, succulent slice of duck and put it in her mouth. It tasted wonderful. She didn't enjoy it, but ate nonetheless. Her mother had brought her up to eat whatever landed in front of her, hungry or not.

The waiter reappeared to clear the starter plates. He returned soon after with a fillet of steak smothered in a blue cheese sauce.

Amira looked at the plate and wondered if they were so different, she and the piece of meat.

Pavel talked between mouthfuls. "Beautiful, articulate, educated. The same can't be said for everyone who gets off those boats."

"Everyone is someone," Amira said, slamming her knife and fork down on the plate. She felt the anger rising in her chest. "But you treat us like no one."

Pavel shifted in his seat. "That's logistical stuff. It's not really my area—"

"Then what *do* you do?" Amira asked, unable to contain herself any longer. "And what do you want with me?"

Pavel paused. He rested his knife and fork on his plate and dabbed his napkin against his lips. "When I see something special, I want it."

"Then you can keep wanting," Amira said, pushing her plate away.

Pavel leaned forward on his elbows. "We're more alike than you think, Amira. We both aspire to a better standard of life. I mean, that *is* why you made the trip, is it not?"

Amira found herself unable to argue his point. Wasn't it what everyone wanted? She pulled the plate towards her, picked up her knife and fork and cut into her steak.

Pavel drank from his wine glass. He put the glass down and leaned in with a smile. "I think you're going to like eating here. The desserts are wonderful."

* * *

Dessert was a chocolate mousse Amira didn't touch. Tony held the door open to the room. Amira entered with Pavel close behind. Tony closed the door, leaving them alone.

Amira stayed away from the bed and the grey sofa at the opposite end of the room. She backed up against the nearest wall.

Pavel strolled towards her. He removed his jacket and tossed it onto the end of the bed. He stopped and circled the palms of both hands over her bare shoulders. He spoke close to her left ear, his breath on her neck. "I find you very attractive, Amira," he said in a half-whisper. "I could make you very comfortable."

Comfortable? Amira found every moment in his presence excruciating.

Pavel put a thumb on her bottom lip, as if expecting her to invite it in. He moved it down to her chin, tilted her head so that their eyes met. Leaned in for a kiss.

Amira turned her head away. She stared anywhere but at him.

Pavel let out a frustrated sigh. "Fine, suit yourself."

"That's it?" Amira said. "You're not going to drug me? Rape me? Put a gun to my head?"

Pavel pulled on his suit jacket. "I'm not one of those thugs on the boat, thank you very much." He adjusted the lapels on his jacket. "Besides, this was merely a dress rehearsal . . . You'll do fine."

"At what?"

"At whatever the clients want. The first one will take you to lunch beforehand."

"Before—?"

"You can wear the same dress," Pavel said. "I'll arrange some more outfits in the meantime."

Amira folded her arms across her chest. "I don't understand."

Pavel put a hand to Amira's cheek. "I'm afraid you'll have to be more accommodating tomorrow. Or else I'll have to be less so." Pavel took a step away, buttoning his jacket. "One p.m. tomorrow. Tony will escort you down."

"I don't care what you told your *client*," Amira said. "I'm not doing it."

Pavel laughed and ran a hand through his hair. "You're beautiful, smart and you can hold a conversation. That makes you valuable . . . But our clients expect the five-star service. So if I have to replace you, I will." Pavel strode towards the door and knocked on the wood. Tony opened the door from the outside. "Work on your enthusiasm in the meantime," Pavel said on his way out. He stopped and turned. "Oh, and I'll have a doctor come in the morning."

"What for?" Amira said.

"Just a standard checkup. Blood, urine, heart rate," Pavel said with a smile. "You've been through a lot, Amira. We want to make sure you're okay."

Pavel left the room. Tony closed the door, leaving Amira alone. She ripped off her high heel shoes, wriggled out of her dress and threw it on the carpet. She ran to the bathroom, lifted the toilet seat and heaved over the bowl. She wanted to throw up the expensive dinner. She couldn't. She washed off her makeup and changed into her pyjamas. After an hour, she tried the door. Tony had locked it with a key from the outside.

She banged on the wood. Screamed again in frustration.

A moment or two later, she calmed down. She rested her forehead against the door and flicked the light switch on the wall. She stood there in the dark, the room tinged blue by moonlight spilling in through the windows. Pavel had told her to spend the night working on her enthusiasm.

Perhaps it wasn't such a bad idea. It might just save her life. But could she go through with it?

She had until lunch the next day to decide.

Chapter 44

I spend the night in the boot of the Volvo in the car park of a motorway services, southwest of London. It's cold and noisy and they don't make sleeping bags long enough for people who are six-five.

At least with the seats down, there's room to stretch out.

During the night, I dream of Amira, the sick young girl, the others trapped in the back of that truck. They suffocate to death while I tap dance with a crocodile outside the doors.

Bloody nonsense.

I wake up to the smell of soap powder. My hair stuck rigid with the stuff. The rear windscreen of the car drips with condensation. My mouth screams for a drink.

I open the boot to a spotless blue sky.

Sunny but chilly. The sporadic roar of motorway traffic. I clamber out of the Volvo and traipse across the car park to the main services building.

It's quiet inside. The usual mix of franchise outposts. The smell of coffee, warm muffins and McDonald's breakfasts. I head straight for a small WHSmiths. They're selling travel stuff. I buy some miniature toiletries and wash myself in the sink of the gents. They've got those ridiculous taps where you need to keep a hand on it at all times. Like you can't be trusted to turn it off when you're done.

I guess some muppets can't.

I clean my upper half with a cloth. I bend over double and wash my hair under the tap. Give it a quick blast under the dryer. I keep it short, so it's dry in no time.

Next up, brekkie. I bypass the McMuffin and go straight for the Big Mac meal and a black coffee.

I return to the Volvo with a bag of sweets and a bottle of water, roll up the sleeping bag and fix the back seats in place

I consult the map I found inside the glove box. Prince's gaff isn't too far away. Only an hour up the road.

If you're gonna raid someone's house, common logic says you're gonna do it at night. He'd have been expecting that, so I decided to rest up, clean up, get my head straight. Hit him when his guard is down.

I pull out of the services, throw a strawberry Starburst in my gob and blast the Volvo down the motorway.

* * *

Typical. The bastard's guard is still up.

I roll past the tall steel gates to Prince's estate. He's got two blokes stood behind 'em. Blokes in casual clothes. Weapons concealed, but they're armed for sure.

I cruise a quarter of a mile down the street. It's lined by high stone walls and bushes, with the occasional millionaire mansion. I pull a U-turn and park up against the kerb. I stick out like a sore dick around here. The only car parked on the road. And somehow I doubt anyone drives a second hand Volvo estate.

Think, Charlie, think.

No one drives a maroon Volvo, no. But they do put their bins out. Bright blue recycling ones lined up for collection. And on the way in, I passed a spotless orange bin truck doing its morning rounds.

Here it is in my rear view mirrors, stopping a hundred metres down.

I run a quick weapons check. Two guns ought to do it. One in each holster. A double strap inside my jacket. I climb out and walk towards the bin lorry as it comes up the street.

It stops while a couple of guys riding the back of it hop off to collect the bins. I open the passenger side door to the cab and climb in.

The driver is wiry and silver-haired. "What, who—"

"I need to borrow your truck," I say, flashing him the butt of a pistol.

The man doesn't argue. He opens his door and jumps down from the cab.

I slide behind the wheel and put it in gear. The truck lurches off along the street, leaving the collectors standing with bins in hand.

I crank it into second. Third. Overtaking my car. Getting some speed up. The roads around here are smooth and wide. I swing out as far as I can to the right, then throw a sharp left as I come up on Prince's driveway.

The thing about bin lorries—they're heavy. Not only

from all the machinery on the back. They're full of recycling too.

I accelerate as fast as it'll go, nose pointed straight at those steel gates.

The two men on guard don't react fast enough. The truck slams through the gates with a bang, a whine and a snapping of metal.

I mow the guards down.

I head towards the house. The windscreen is cracked and half the gate dragging and sparking over the driveway. More guards come running. Gunfire rattles into the side of the truck. I duck low behind the wheel and head straight for the main entrance.

I'm half thinking of ploughing through the front of it. But the closer I get, the more I realise he's built a fake bloody castle for himself. Stone walls, turrets and big oak doors with iron studs. The whole ridiculous lot.

There'd only be one winner. And it doesn't collect empty tins of caviar.

I pull the wheel to the right and slam on the brakes. The truck skids to a stop. I bail out of the driver's side and run around the back of the lorry. You could play snooker on the plush green lawns of Prince's place. They sweep down towards the road. A pair of suited and booted guards come running up the grass with automatic weapons.

The only cover they've got is a bank of pink rhododendrons. I whirl out from around the truck and hit one with a round. He spins into a bush. His mate returns fire. I double-back around to the front of the truck and hit him in the neck. He drops to the turf, too. I pause a second and see the damage done. The gates lie in pieces. So do the men guarding 'em.

I make for the entrance. The front door's locked, so I pick up a large clay pot with a plant in it. I tip out the plant and the soil. It's bloody heavy, but I heave it onto a shoulder and hurl it through a front window. A huge pane of stained glass crashes down. I climb into a large dining room with polished wooden floors, high ceilings and a long oak table and chairs.

The guy must be into history or something, because everything is medieval and up its own arse.

I come out of the dining room into a grand hallway with stone flooring. It's lined by tall iron candelabras and a varnished wooden staircase to my left.

Another goon in a suit comes running. I catch him by surprise, grabbing a candelabra and whacking him in the face with the base. I drop the make-do weapon and march down a corridor. I poke my head in a few rooms.

There's a large, luxurious living room with wooden beams overhead. Another room with a snooker table. And last but no less pompous, a library with a huge stone fireplace full of crackling, glowing logs. It has a wall full of old books I doubt the fucker's ever read and a desk on ornamental brass legs.

I catch Eddie Prince stood by an antique chest of drawers. He's got a hand inside one of 'em. He pulls out a silver revolver and checks the barrel.

"Don't bother, Eddie," aiming my gun at him.

He sets the revolver down and steps away slow from the drawers. He's an average-sized man. Bald and freckled on top with a Costa-Del-Crime tan and what looks like a facelift since I saw him last. He wears tartan slippers and a matching wool dressing gown left open. A pair of sky-blue pyjama bottoms and a white t-shirt underneath.

He throws his arms open like I'm a long lost son. "Breaker," he says in his gravelled Essex voice. "What a nice surprise. See your communication style hasn't changed much. You should've called ahead."

I keep the gun trained on him. He's a slippery eel. I can see the cogs turning in his potato-shaped head.

I last worked for Eddie Prince around six years ago. Remember that north-south civil war I mentioned? Eddie Prince was the southern boss. A major player back then. Famous for cutting the throats of his enemies. Letting them bleed to a slow death.

Prince Eddie, most people call him. A top of the line arsehole, I call him.

"So Charlie," Prince says. "How much is this gonna cost me?"

"Why does everyone assume I'm after their money?"

"Because you usually are. And I could do with a new fixer, now Randall's on the slab."

"He dead then?" I ask.

"Got the call this morning. Police found him swinging. Dave called me n'all. Told me to expect you."

"Well don't reach for your chequebook. I'm not looking for work."

"What then? Revenge? I had nothing to do with that thing at the building site."

"I bet you know who did, though. Don't you?"

"No idea what you're talking about."

"That's what everyone says. Right up until I find out they do."

Prince's face darkens. His nostrils flare. He takes a step forward. "Are you threatening me, son? 'Cause I'm trying to be nice here."

"Most people are nice when there's a gun on 'em."

Prince paces left and right. "This isn't some small-time arsehole you're talking to here. This is Eddie Prince. Prince fucking Eddie. I'm the ghost and the darkness, son." Prince works himself into a right frenzy. "I'm a fucking man-eater. King of the jungle. The antichrist and Jesus Christ. You're dealing with royalty here, sunshine. So if you're gonna shoot me, you'd better make sure of it. Or I'll click my fingers and that ugly head of yours'll be rolling around my lawn while Lucky uses it as a chew toy. You filthy piece of thick northern shit."

Prince wipes a string of spit off his chin.

I lower my weapon. Tuck it in my holster. "I'm not gonna shoot you, Eddie."

The old slap-head calms himself down. Sniffs, face flushed red. "Yeah, that's what I thought."

I grab the handle of a brass poker lodged in the fire. I pull it out and thrust the hot, glowing end into Prince's guts. He screams. I let go of the handle. He staggers back against his desk, the poker still in him.

Now we'll see if he talks.

Chapter 45

I peer around the back of Prince Eddie. The tip of the poker sticks out the other side. "Well look at that," I say. "It went all the way through."

It takes a minute for Prince to stop yelping. His t-shirt stains with blood. I wait for the screaming to quiet to a whimper. He holds onto the poker handle, trembling, bent over the desk.

"The antichrist, my arse," I say, lowering my voice and leaning in close to his ear. "Who's heading up the operation? I know it's not you. You're not bloody capable."

"You don't know who you're going after," he says, voice breaking. "They're rabid dogs. They'll tear you to fucking pieces."

"Then it's in your interests to tell me, isn't it?"

Prince doesn't crack.

I hear feet running into the room. It's Marla, Prince's wife. White satin dressing gown and fluffy pink slippers. Dyed black hair, fake lips and drawn-on eyebrows.

"Eddie?" she says. *"Jesus, Eddie!"* She rushes over to her husband. *"What have you done to him?"*

"Just a misunderstanding," I say.

"I'll phone an ambulance," says Marla.

I snatch the cordless phone away from her. "Not until hubby here talks."

"I don't care what you do to me," Prince says through gritted teeth. "I'm not saying shit."

"What about your wife?" I say, picking up a letter opener off the desk. "You care what happens to her?" I drive the letter opened into Marla's right shoulder, a few inches above the fake boob. She wails. I twist. She wails some more, blood pouring out of the wound.

Prince isn't happy. *"Get off her you fucking animal!"*

I hold up the phone in my free hand. "I can call her an ambulance right now, Eddie."

He shakes his head. "They'll kill us both anyway."

I keep twisting. Marla keeps screaming. "The less you talk Eddie, the more I twist."

"Please, Eddie!" Marla cries.

I sing the words to "Let's Twist Again" by Chubby Checker.

Indeed I do twist again. Left. Right.

Until the great Prince Eddie finally breaks. *"Stop! Stop! What do you wanna know?"*

"Everything," I say, taking my hand off the letter opener.

I find a pad of posh writing paper on the desk, along with a gold ballpoint pen. I click out the nib, pull Eddie over to the pad and shove the pen in his hand. "Names, details, how they operate, where they keep the refugees."

Eddie hesitates. His hand shaking.

"Come on Eddie, Marla's bleeding out over here."

"I'm thinking! I'm thinking! I've got a fucking red-hot poker in me."

I yank the letter opener out of Marla's shoulder. Blood spatters the desk. She yelps and puts a hand to the wound.

"Now she's bleeding out faster," I say.

"Alright, alright," Prince says. "But I don't know everything."

As Eddie writes, something occurs to me. "On second thoughts," I say, dialling 999. I call an ambulance. Toss the phone in the fire. "You'll be alright love," I say to Marla. "Put a towel against the wound and find somewhere to sit down. It's a plush area, so the ambulance ought to get here before you snuff it." I grab Prince by the lapel of his dressing gown. "*You* . . . You're coming with me."

I tear the top sheet of paper off the pad. I drag Prince away from the desk. Marla screams and wails. Eddie too. I ignore the pair of 'em and march him out of the house. I snatch a black key fob from a blue ceramic bowl in the hallway.

I open one of the huge front doors and we walk down the steps. "I've given you what you wanted," Prince says.

"I can't be sure you're not lying."

"Come on, Charlie. You know me—"

"Yeah, that's the problem."

The key fob has a silver Rolls Royce logo on the back. I look left and right as we come out of the house. I see a shiny black Roller parked up a short walk to the left of the house. The locks pop as we approach. I open the rear passenger door and shove Prince inside.

The poker catches on the seat as he gets in. He cries out. I slam the door, hurry round to the driver's side and get in behind the wheel.

"Bloody hell, it's like The Savoy in here."

I'm not exaggerating either. The front of the cabin is as big as a living room, full of hand-stitched cream leather and walnut.

There's even an umbrella holder.

A bloody umbrella holder.

"Right Mr Prince," I say, starting the engine, looking at his scrawl on the paper. "Where can I find this place?"

"What am I, a fucking TomTom?" he says.

"The more you argue, the longer you'll have that poker stuck inside you."

He arranges himself sideways on the backseat. "Put it in the bastard sat nav," he says, wincing.

I take his advice. The route pops up. I steer the Rolls down the driveway, around the broken gates and mangled bodies of the men I mowed over. There are two streaks of blood leading all the way down to the front entrance. It's a messy business sometimes.

I steer out onto the road. The neighbours out in their dressing gowns, gawping for England.

"Fuckin' hell," Prince says, "There's blood on the leather."

Chapter 46

"You stabbed him with a poker?" Cassie says, pulling a face in the passenger seat.

"Will you stop appearing like that, Cass? Shits me up every time."

"What do you want, a text?"

"Might as well," I say, "You spend enough time on that phone of yours. And the slaphead in the back has done a lot worse than stab people with a poker."

"Two wrongs, Dad."

"Stop whining," I say. "You want me to sort these traffickers out or not?"

"Not if you're gonna stab innocent women with letter openers."

I can't help laughing at that one. "*Innocent?* She once ordered a hit on a traffic warden."

"Yeah, but—"

"She wears animal fur and conflict diamonds," I say.

"Oh," Cass says, changing tune. "Well in that case . . ."

"Sure you don't wanna stop off at the looney bin while

we're out?" Prince asks from the backseat. "Northern nutter."

"I can drop you off right here if you want," I say.

"You do realise you're driving to your own funeral." Prince says, talking through the pain, holding the poker steady in the wound. "If I were you I'd turn around now. Drop me off at the hospital. No hard feelings."

"And why would the notorious Prince Eddie be scared of another gang?"

"Because they're not like us," Prince says. "We've got standards."

I laugh.

"It's true," he says.

"Then why get into bed with 'em?" I ask, steering the Rolls along a country road, through sweeping farmland dotted with cattle.

"Times are tough," Prince says.

"The price of fake castles gone up?"

"People can get it all online nowadays," Prince says. "Coke, hookers, betting, stolen goods. You need to diversify."

"And that means ripping off desperate people?" I say, turning off onto a narrow lane.

"Oh sorry, Florence Nightingale. What other kind of business is there?"

I let his comment bounce. Keep him talking. I need him alive as we roll through woodland either side of a small side road. "So what do these people need you for?"

"Logistics. Contacts. Local knowledge," Prince says. "We

pay off the Old Bill and customs. Move the merchandise from port. We take our cut and they do the rest. Easy money if you ask me . . . On the left here."

An old army barracks pops up at us out of the trees. Long, high walls with rolls of barbed wire on top and surrounded by ploughed fields. There's a solid steel gate painted army green across the entrance. Signs plastered all over the gate: *Property of VX Holdings*.

"Let me guess, VX Holdings is one of yours."

"Government cuts, got the place for a song," Prince says, shifting forward on the backseat. Face turning white from the wound. I stabbed him in just the right place. No organs or major arteries in the way. The poker holding everything in place and a closed wound stopping him bleeding out too quick.

"What's the set-up inside?" I ask.

"How should I know?" Prince says. "I'm the landlord, that's all."

"Right," I say, opening my door. "Well we'll have to wing it, as usual." I get out of the car and open one of the rear doors to the Rolls. I drag Prince out.

"What are you doing?" he says.

"I need you out of sight," I say, opening the boot.

"You can't be serious—I've given you what you need. Now *I* need a fucking surgeon."

I force him inside the boot and slam the lid. It catches on the end of the poker. Bloody thing won't shut. I try it a couple more times. Prince yelping. It closes on the third go.

I get back in the car and jam a fresh clip into both

handguns. I holster the pair of 'em inside my jacket and drive up to the front gate.

There's a steel pole sticking out of the ground with a small metal box to talk into. I push a button on the front of the box.

"What?" a foreign voice asks. Eastern European. Tinny and crackling.

"I've got Mr Prince."

There's a discreet security camera to the top left of the gate. The windows of the Rolls are tinted. I hope this works.

"What does he want?" the voice in the box asks. "We weren't expecting him."

"He owns the place, pal."

"And we pay rent. Put him on."

"He's on the phone, mate . . . Look, I'm just the driver. You wanna upset the man? 'Cause I don't."

There's a long, crackled pause. The sound of a buzzer. The heavy clunk of the gate unlocking. The whir of a motor as it slides to the right. It reveals a long, wide stretch of concrete. It leads up to a three-storey brick building with white window frames. The building is rundown. A bank of overgrown grass in front.

No sign of any armed guards.

I pull up to the right in front of the grass bank. I keep the engine running and wait.

A fire exit door opens and out steps a man in a dark-blue body warmer and grey sweats. He has an automatic rifle strapped over a shoulder. He walks down a path to the car and appears on the driver's side. He raps his knuckles on the glass.

I wind down the window a few inches. "Mr Prince will be a minute."

The guard's eyes are bloodshot. His face the colour of ash. Drawn and unshaven. Like he's been up for three nights straight and deprived of sunlight. His nostrils bright red. Either he's got a cold, or a habit.

"Out," the guard says.

"Alright," I say, opening the driver door. I step out and stretch. Breathe in the country air.

The guard isn't the biggest of guys but he's grizzled and mean-looking. I don't like the sign of grey in a man's beard. It means he's experienced. Means I've gotta be careful.

"Turn around," he says. "Hands on the car."

I yawn and turn. "Okay mate, take it easy."

The guard shoves me in the back. I place both hands on the cool, smooth paintwork of the Rolls.

"You carrying?" the guard asks.

"Who isn't?" I say. "Inside the jacket, left and right."

I feel the weight of both guns removed from the holsters. Hear him detach the clips and slip the guns back in, light and harmless.

I turn my head and see him slide the clips in the front pockets of his body warmer. He has a small black radio attached to his collar. He talks foreign into it.

He taps me on the shoulder. "Get your boss out."

I take my hands off the roof and knock on the rear window. "Mr Prince?" I wait, turn and smile. The guard is behind me, but keeping his distance. He doesn't look impressed. I knock again on the glass. "Mr Prince . . .

They're ready for you." I wait another few seconds. Turn to the guard. "Sorry about this." I open the passenger door and duck my head inside. "Look Mr Prince, he's insisting that I—Okay, Mr Prince."

"What's happening?" the guard asks, trying to get a look in.

Unfortunately for him, my fat arse takes up the entire door frame. I pull a backup weapon from the rear pocket of the driver seat.

"Sorry pal," I say, spinning fast. I get the drop on the guard. The barrel of my pistol to his forehead. I take his rifle and slide it off his shoulder.

A voice on the radio says something. Don't understand a word, but sounds like a question. A status check.

"Tell him everything's fine," I whisper. "In English . . . And be convincing."

"All clear," the guard says. "Prince wants to look at—"

"Um, land drainage," I say.

"Land drainage," the guard says.

"Copy," the voice on the radio says.

"Cheers mate," I say to the guard. I strike him in the side of the temple with the butt of his own weapon. He goes down. I hook his rifle over my shoulder and tuck my backup in the waist of my jeans. I lock the Rolls and drag the guard backwards up the path, in through the side door of the main building. I leave the guy slumped in a dark corner, retrieve my clips and walk through a set of wooden doors with small windows.

I continue down a set of dark and dank corridors.

Nothing but the echo of my boots. And an annoying dripping sound.

Further along, I hear a faint murmur. A cough. I stick my head around a door and see a dark room full of single cots covered with military issue blankets. A couple with squirming bodies underneath. The room stinks of stale sweat.

I move on, to another set of doors. I hear a voice on the other side. The same language the guard was talking. I push the door open a crack. See a big, burly guy with shaved black hair, jabbering on the phone by a stairwell. He's smoking. Pacing. Laughing like a girl. He walks towards the door, turns and strolls the other way. I push the door open slow and creep up behind him.

He must feel a presence, because he half turns. It's too late for him. I grab a hand full of rough stubbled face. Another of his fat, clammy neck. I twist the neck. Hear it snap.

I crush the phone under my boot as I step over his body. I push through the next door and come to a large, empty canteen. Dirty plates fill the tables, with leftover slop and flies buzzing around the place. Christ, this place is awful. Someone needs to open a bloody window.

I move on to the far end of the ground floor. I'm starting to wonder if Prince shafted me with the wrong information. But the presence of armed guards means there must be something here worth looking into.

And here comes another one. A fat lump with a short, black semi-mohawk.

As he exits a set of large oak doors at the end of the

corridor, there's a brief murmur of activity behind him. He coughs as he strolls, weapon over shoulder. Scratching his crotch. Dredging up a ball of phlegm and spitting it sideways onto the floor.

I wait inside a doorway. As he passes by, I slam him in the head with the rifle. He staggers against the wall. I hit him again and he's out. I pull him by the loose waist of his baggy blue jeans. I leave him inside a room: an old office with a desk and two chairs and an army recruiting poster on the wall.

I close the door on the guy and head to the place he just came from at the end of the corridor. There's a sign saying *Gym Hall*.

The doors to the Gym Hall have chunky brass handles. I pull one open a foot. Raise my weapon. Slip through the gap, finger on trigger. I'm faced by a large hall with high windows and basketball hoops at either end. Weak shafts of dusty daylight break in from above. Power cables snake across the gym floor. Table lights extend from the sockets. The lights stand on long wooden tables arranged in four rows in the centre of the hall.

The room is a hive of quiet activity. A dozen or more people from all parts of the world. They're stripped to their underwear with noses and mouths covered by white masks. Hair tucked up in clear plastic shower caps. Most of them are men, with a few women thrown in.

I scan the gym left to right. No one seems to have noticed me slip inside. I sidestep along the near wall, counting scumbags.

I see two of 'em.

One sits at a desk, glued to a laptop in the far left corner. The other stares at an iPad in the far right.

What's the point of this little setup, you might ask?

From the bulk packs of aspirin, lidocaine, phenacetin and baking soda stacked towards the near wall, I'd say they're cutting up kilo bags of coke. I also see they've got laxatives and worming tablets ready to go.

In my experience of these places, they'll cut the coke with just about anything they can get their hands on.

They've got the workers making up small plastic pouches of the stuff. They open the coke. Divide it up. Mix it with a blend of stimulants and painkillers. Bulk it with sodas and powders. Then weigh it and syphon it off into these pouches.

That's how you know the fine white powder is shitty quality.

And I'm willing to bet those workers are slave labour.

As I lurk in the shadows, planning my next move, I notice a third guard I didn't see before. He walks between rows, inspecting the work. He hasn't seen me yet. I could put him down right now. Then the other two. But there are people in the way. Automatic rifles and a room full of panicking bodies don't tend to mix well. I slide the strap to the back of my shoulder and reach inside my jacket. I pull out a handgun and aim it at the guard walking the rows.

He's a string bean with long ginger hair and a face like a rat. He stands over a short Arabic man and knocks a steel weighing scale over. *"You're using too much!"* he shouts in his face. He brings his rifle up to the man's head. Digs it in his skull. The other workers keep cutting. No one daring to look up. The Arabic shakes and holds his head. The guard yells some more.

It draws the attention of the other two guards. The one with the iPad spots me. He shouts and points my way, snatching his rifle off a table.

I glance at the other two guards. Their eyes on me. Somehow, I don't think they'll give a crap about cutting those workers to ribbons in the crossfire.

But it's either shoot first, or die.

Chapter 47

I shoot first.

Into the air.

The workers cry out in fear. They duck low to their tables. Before the lanky, ginger guard can take aim, I level my pistol and put a bullet between his eyes.

More screams as his body hits the deck. I'm moving low and fast across the gym hall. The whole place lighting up with machine gun fire. I dive behind the stacks of pills and powders.

I stay low as bullets puncture each pack, spitting out small white clouds of dust. I hold my fire a few seconds, letting the clouds rise and thicken into one. I can't see the guards, but they can't see me, either.

The gunfire drops off, the echoes die down.

I crouch and turn on the balls of my feet. I listen to the guards calling out to each other in their own language.

It gives me a fix on their position. Both still in their corners.

It's do or die time. I count to three, rush out of the cloud and straighten up. I shoot twice and catch the guard with the iPad once in the head. I see the blood spray from his skull.

I whirl around and fire, almost blind through the cloud.

There's a brief burst of return fire. A flash, a bang, but as I advance out of the cloud, I see the remaining guard is down. I pad myself up and down for bullet holes, surprised to be alive.

The workers are silent, hunkering under the tables. I do a lap of the gym, checking on iPad guy first. Yep, he's dead. Can't do much with half your brain missing.

The ginger one is a goner too. A pool of blood forming around his body. I hurry to the table with the laptop on it. The guard twitches. He bleeds from the chest, his weapon smoking on the lacquered wooden flooring, out of his reach.

I take a seat behind the laptop. The guy bleeding out by my feet is more than hired muscle. He was doing numbers work—a spreadsheet full of figures.

Shipments, supplies and cashflow.

I don't understand any of the shit, but I guess it'll make for good evidence. I minimise the spreadsheet and nose around the desktop for more dirt.

I keep an eye on the gym entrance. If there are any goons left in the building, they've got to have heard the gunfight.

I click on a database file that says *Labour*. A long list of potted profiles opens up. I scroll down the list: mugshots of people against a white wall. A number and location next to each face: Woodington or Silvertown.

I look for Amira. She isn't there.

I get up and walk over to the workers. They're removing their masks, rising to their feet. Unsure who I am or what I want.

"Does anyone remember me?" I ask. "From the truck?"

They look at each other. Shit, I bet most of them don't speak English.

I scan their faces. Worried. Haunted. Exhausted. I recognise one of them. Two, maybe, but I can't be sure.

A man steps forward. "I remember."

"Do you know what happened to Amira?" I ask.

"They took her," he says.

"Where to?"

"Another place."

"What other place?"

"They take some of the women. They don't come back."

I hear the guard I hit in the chest groaning. Faint, but alive. I march over to him. He's conscious, reaching for that rifle. I step on his hand. He cries out. I kneel down and take a closer look at his chest. The wound isn't fatal. Looks as if it passed through and missed anything vital.

I put my gun to his head. "Where else are you keeping people?"

He coughs, but doesn't talk.

I cock the pistol. "Where?"

"No English," he says.

I jab a thumb in his bullet wound. It's hot and "minging" as Cassie would put it.

The guy screams in pain, especially when I turn my thumb. His eyes do the talking, moving towards the laptop.

She's gotta be on there. I return to the computer. Click on a few files.

Out of the corner of an eye, I see the guy's hand going for the rifle again. I continue to click through, but aim my gun behind me. I shoot him in the heart.

I don't have to look round to see he's dead. I click on another file. A second list of people. I scroll down. I fly past her and stop dead. I scroll back up. There she is. Amira. Number 7564. Silvertown.

The laptop has the internet, so I hop onto Google. Type in the name of the place. As I do, the gym doors open. Another goon bursts in, dressed in boxers and a t-shirt. He hesitates, trying to make sense of the mess. I snatch my handgun off the desk and drop him.

The workers jump at the sound. The goon collapses, his body trapped between the doors.

I realise I've got to get us out of here. I shut the laptop and rip out the connections. I holster my handgun and pull the rifle over my shoulder, the laptop under one arm. I pick the nearest dead guard's rifle from the floor and approach the workers.

"Anyone know how to fire one of these?"

The man who remembers me nods," I was a soldier."

"What's your name?" I say.

"Malik."

"Well here you go, Malik." I toss him the rifle. "Follow me."

Malik and the rest follow on, still a little suspicious of me. But who can blame 'em?

I drag the fallen goon away from the doors and lead the group into the corridor.

I tell them to stay behind me. I motion to stick tight to the wall. We move in single file. We pass through the doors where I left the guy with his neck snapped, drawing immediate fire. It's coming from two guards on the stairs. I pull back behind the doors. The old solid oak sucks up a round of bullets. I push out again and return fire.

Our attackers look as if they've rolled out of bed. They scramble for cover. Malik joins me and we pin 'em down while the others run through the next set of doors. We follow after 'em. Malik knows his stuff. How to shoot. How to move. We back up as we go, either side of the corridor. I signal to him—each of us hide inside a doorway. As soon as those guards appear through the doors, we spin out into the corridor and cut 'em down.

We catch up to the others, down the grass embankment and out onto the driveway of the barracks. The refugees blink into the daylight like they've never seen the sun. Even an April sun lost behind scattered clouds.

I throw the laptop on the passenger seat of the Rolls.

Now I've got 'em out, I'm not sure what to do with 'em. I can't take 'em with me and they can't make it out of here on foot. Meanwhile, the guys running the operation here are bound to have called their bosses.

And who knows if there are more of those goons hanging around the place, waking up from shift naps?

There's only one thing I can think to do.

Chapter 48

We wait inside the front gate to the barracks. A short distance from the main building.

If there were any more guards left alive in the building, they would have come running out of there by now.

Fire will do that to people. Even a small one like this.

It was easy to do. A can of turps and a cloth in a storage cupboard. The strike of a match.

It flames orange out of two ground floor windows. Toxic smoke spoiling the air.

I started it at the end furthest from the gym hall. I want that intact for when they get here.

And here *they* are.

The faint cry of sirens on the breeze. Louder and louder still.

I motion to the rest of our group to stay back out of the way. I take the spare rifle off Malik and jog out through the entrance. I head left, to where I parked the Rolls up by the side of the road.

I climb behind the wheel and bide my time. As a pair of

fire engines charge in down the narrow country lane, I start the car. I let the trucks flash by into the barracks.

An ambulance is hot on their heels. I called it in separate to make sure they sent one out. Whichever got here first, it wouldn't have mattered. Just so long as they got here before more of those traffickers.

Whoever they've dispatched to deal with the uprising, they'll soon turn around when they see the emergency services.

The pigs won't be far behind either, so I pull into the road, through the canopy of trees and out onto the country lanes. I drive at speed until I've cleared the area. I stop in the entrance to a farmer's field. I pop the boot and walk around the back of the Rolls. I open the lid and find Eddie Prince alive.

White as a sheet, but alive. I help him out of the boot.

"Took your fucking time," Prince says, voice weakening by the minute.

"Silvertown," I say. "One of your places?"

"No, it's a docks down West Ham way. Why?"

"Ah, nothing. You've done your bit, Eddie."

"At fucking last," he says. We stand looking at each other. "Well come on then," Prince says. "Take me to hospital."

I check my watch. "Yeah, you'll have to make your own way there."

"My own way—?"

"I saw a bus stop a mile back. Should be one every hour or so, I reckon."

I hand him a fiver.

"You snivelling shit," he says. "I'm gonna die out here."

"Not if you get a wriggle on," I say, returning to the driver's door of the Rolls. Prince stands in disbelief. I clap my hands. "Go on. Chop, chop."

I jump inside, pull the door shut and apply the central locking. Prince pulls at the door handle to the back seats. He pounds the glass as I pull away. I see him going berserk in the rear view mirror. But he soon runs out of expletives. In the distance, he turns and staggers towards the bus stop.

At least *I think* there was a bus stop.

I pull out my phone. Call up Detective Clarke. "I want to meet," I say, glancing at the laptop on the passenger seat. "Got something else for you. Something big."

* * *

We meet somewhere different this time. The top level of a multi-storey. A view over the sloping, slate-grey rooftops of London. As usual, we're in the grottier end.

The roof of the car park is empty. Detective Clarke waits for me in the centre. I brake to a sudden stop alongside him, my window down.

Clarke winds down his own. A scowl on his face. "What the hell have you done with Eddie Prince?"

"Relax, he's in one piece."

"Where exactly?"

"Depends if he caught a bus or not. If he didn't, you might find him in the fields, out Surrey way."

"Alive?"

"Well if he's not, you can tick him off your list. One less dickhead to worry about."

Clarke rubs a hand over his face. "We were talking him into being a snitch. I think we were close. Now his wife's in hospital and there are four dead bodies on his lawn."

"They shot at me first. What was I supposed to do? Wave a hanky?"

"Not steal a bin lorry and ram it through his front gates."

"You wanted this," I say. "You got it."

"Yeah, well there'll be no one left to prosecute at this rate."

"No one left to exploit refugees, either."

"What I mean is, we won't be able to use them to get at the senior figures. The real operators."

"Then you'd better get off your arse and start helping."

Clarke sips on a takeaway coffee. "You know we can't go around kicking doors in. Why do you think I let you loose on this?"

"Then don't complain when it gets tasty. Christ, you coppers. You want your bloody cake, don't you?"

"Didn't think it'd be this public. The papers have got hold of it. Local TV, too. They're asking a lot of questions and we don't have any answers . . . First, Randall's found dead. Now this. What's your plan, Charlie?"

"Moving up the food chain," I say. "You had the call yet?"

"About what?"

"The barracks."

"What barracks?"

I reach over to the passenger seat and grab the laptop. I hand it over.

Clarke takes it. "What now?"

"Hard evidence." I hand him Prince's scribbled note with the address of the barracks. "There's a crew putting out a small fire. They've probably found the coke and the slave labour by now. If you get you get your arse in gear, you might get there early enough to put your name on it."

Clarke starts the engine on his car.

"One more thing, Columbo," I say. "I've got something else for you. A second location, down the docks. You tie this one to the barracks and you've got a case, with or without Prince Eddie. Once you've bagged and tagged at the barracks, you can kick in the doors of this other place—"

Clarke holds up a hand. Stops me dead. "There's not gonna be a raid, Charlie."

"What? Are you thick or something? I'm handing it you on a silver platter. On a bloody velvet cushion."

"It's not that simple. It takes patience, politics."

"It takes the piss, that's what."

Clarke swallows another mouthful of coffee. "For a man who doesn't give a toss, you seem awfully passionate."

"There's a way to do business," I say. "And this isn't it."

Clarke says nothing.

I shake my head at him. "Never mind, I'll see to it myself." I start the engine. "Get yourself to those barracks. We'll see how patient you are then."

For the first time, Clarke seems to clock that I'm driving a Rolls. "Is that Prince's motor?"

"Bloody hell Sherlock, nothing gets past you." I put the Rolls in gear.

"Promise me you won't make a mess," Clarke says.

I can't help laughing. "I'm just warming up," I say, stepping on the accelerator.

I drive across the rooftop car park and spiral down to street level. The last thing I wanna do is go after these bastards alone, but I'm damned if I'm leaving Amira and the others to rot.

I tap on the onboard computer screen. Type the second location in the sat nav. I set off towards Silvertown.

Chapter 49

I step inside a greasy spoon full of dockers between shifts.

It's warm, noisy and smells of bacon and eggs. A radio plays pop music. The colour scheme is white tables and green chairs.

There's a pile of coats hung up on a rack as you enter the café. A large, mousy-haired woman behind the counter in a green apron. Forearms like hams. She's a cheerful soul and fixes me up a bacon butty and a cup of tea. I take a seat across from a table where four dock workers demolish a fry up each. They talk in four-letter words. Who beat who in the football. How many pints they sunk at the weekend.

I eat the sandwich. I like my bacon crispy. But it doesn't matter how many times you tell 'em, these gaffs always undercook it. I pull a rubbery piece of fat out of my gob. I sip on my brew. Jesus Christ, what did she do? Wave the tea bag at it?

I open up the butty and squirt on some ketchup. I slap the top piece of bread down and get sauce on my fingers. As I lick it off, I notice the bloke nearest to me scratching his crotch. He's a young lad with shaved hair and tattoos. There he goes again. Scratch, scratch, scratch. That's the third time he's done it inside a minute.

Yeah, he's the fella I'm looking for.

I lean over and tap him on the shoulder. "Hey, pal. You know where a bloke can sow a few oats around here?"

"Depends," he says, turning in his seat. "What type you after?"

"There's more than one type?"

A guy with long, greased-back grey hair sneers at me. "He means, are you a bender?"

"Not unless your mum's a fella," I say. "Come to think of it, she did ask for it up the shit-box. Maybe it was your old man I was shagging."

The four blokes laugh.

The lad with the shaven head lowers his voice. "What I mean is, you into pale or dark? Young or younger?"

"I kinda like the exotic type," I say.

"Then you want Cristina."

"Who's that?" I ask.

The four blokes break into laughter again.

"Ask for Nabil. Say Mickey sent you."

"Alright, will do."

Mickey slaps me on the arm. "That's twenty per cent off my next one. Nice one geez."

I finish the rest of my sandwich. A big old bloke behind me gets to his feet with a groan. He heads to the toilet, taking his newspaper with him.

He leaves an empty plate behind him, stained with swirls of

egg yolk and ketchup. And more importantly, a black woollen hat. I look around me and snatch it off the table. I down the rest of the tea. Bloody awful, but this vigilante lark is thirsty work.

I search for a coat on the rack. One that'll fit. The trick to nicking is not to rush it. I check the length of a sleeve next to my arm and snatch it off the peg.

I open the flimsy café door and step outside. The docks are proper blue collar down here. The city lot live and work further up and over the river in shiny glass buildings like Canary Wharf. No, here it's all tugboats, freighters, shipping containers and giant cranes.

Dockers go about their work and trucks load up with pallets fresh off the boats.

I stand outside the greasy spoon and pull on the stolen coat. I zip it up and prick the collars. I put the hat on and wear it low over my forehead. I dig my hands in my pockets and hunch my shoulders.

I walk a hundred metres up the dock. There's a white ship with a blue hull at the water's edge, yellowing around the edges and moored by giant ropes.

It says *Cristina* on the back. It's the length of a small ferry. Not quite as tall or wide, but big enough to sail a long way with a lot of cargo. I don't see any activity on deck. Just a lone man hanging around dressed much the same as me.

He nods as I approach him. He's dark-skinned and small with a mess of curly black hair.

"You Nabil?" I ask. "Mickey pointed me your way."

The guy looks at me through letterbox eyes. "Not seen you before."

"I'm new, transferred from Liverpool."

The guy rolls his tongue inside his bottom lip. "It's two hundred. You got the money?"

I reach in my pocket for my wallet.

"Not here," he says, checking the coast both ways. "Inside."

He leads me up a narrow set of white steps. They extend over the lapping brown water onto the deck of the ship.

"Mind your head," the guy says, as we enter through a low-hanging doorway.

I hear him too late and nut the steel frame.

It hurts, but I act cool, following him down a set of suspended steel steps. We make a couple of twists and turns and into an office. It has a small porthole window, a desk with a computer on top and a freestanding grey safe in the far corner. The desk has a drawer. He opens it and takes out a sheet of laminated paper.

He walks around to the front of the desk. Hands me the laminated sheet. "Take your pick."

I scan down a list of photographs. Shots of women stood against a white wall. Some of them Arabic. One of them Amira.

I point at Amira's photograph. "That one," I say.

The guy hesitates. "One moment." He picks up the receiver of a black telephone next to the computer monitor. He hits a speed dial number and holds the receiver to his ear. I pace around on the spot, acting casual.

Nabil talks in another language. The same language the guard at the barracks spoke in. He returns the receiver to the handset. "Okay," he says. "But you have to wait."

I check my watch. "How long? My shift starts in an hour."

"Twenty minutes," the guy says. "Or you can choose another."

"No, I'll wait," I say, handing him the sheet. "I like this one."

Nabil looks at me like he's waiting for something.

"Oh, the money. Of course." I pull out my wallet. I count out a couple of hundred in twenties. I hand it over. "Here you go, pal."

Nabil recounts it and pockets the cash. "You can wait here," he says, motioning to a row of three chairs against the wall. He leaves the office without saying a word.

The chairs are blue and hard on the arse cheeks. I sit on one for twenty minutes, watching a clock on the wall behind the desk.

Nabil reappears in the doorway. "Follow me," he says.

I get up and follow him through another series of cramped corridors and down a second staircase. We continue to a fat steel door. He swings it open and invites me in. I'm greeted by a large cargo hold bathed in murky red light. And full of small cubicles: beds behind blue hospital curtains. Two rows of ten.

We walk along the aisle between cubicles.

Some curtains are open, others drawn closed.

I catch sight of young, naked women lying motionless in bed, hooked up to what I reckon must be morphine drips

We pass by a couple of punters along the way. One, an old dock worker with wiry white hair, zipping up. The other, a middle-aged city type in a suit, zipping down.

The place stinks of sweat and stale jizz. It makes my stomach churn.

To my surprise, the guy doesn't drop me off at a cubicle. We walk straight past 'em, to the end of the cargo hold. Through another ridiculously low doorway.

After a sharp right, he stops at a door. "Sorry about the wait. I've arranged a room for you."

"Very kind," I say, wanting to keep him sweet.

He almost manages a smile as he pulls the door open. I step inside.

Amira sits on the edge of a bed against the far wall, long dark hair hanging down over her face. Her body naked, dirty and bruised. Puncture marks in the soft skin between bicep and forearm.

I swallow my anger. Gotta play along.

"You've got fifteen minutes," Nabil says, before disappearing through the door.

I approach the bed. "Amira," I say. She doesn't respond. "Hey, Amira." I put two fingers under her chin and lift her head. I push her lank hair off her face.

The face is vaguely similar. But it's not Amira. She stares at me with nobody-home eyes. The lights barely on. Drool escapes from the corners of her mouth. I shake her by the arms. "Hey, wake up. You know a woman called Amira?" I shake her again. She's loose as a rag-doll. I let her go. Her head drops and that line of drool breaks off and spats on the floor.

Shit. That's Plan A burned to a cinder.

I'm rethinking my options when I hear boots on metal behind me.

Three tall shadows spill across the wall.

I don't even have time to turn around.

Chapter 50

"Remember," Tony had said in his deep southern accent. "It's this or the ship."

Amira had shook her arm from his grip, but entered the restaurant with grace and poise.

She'd taken a seat across from a silver-haired man with a tanned complexion and a tailored pin stripe suit. His name was Terence Rowbottom. *Lord* Terence Rowbottom. A jovial man with a refined manner.

Amira had spoken politely. She smiled through a light risotto. Feigned fascination in his stories about the House of Lords and the various people he knew.

She'd lied about where she was from—Lebanon—as instructed.

She'd also accepted Lord Rowbottom's offer of a large glass of white wine. Even forced herself to laugh along with his racist, sexist humour.

Now, it was time to return to the room, at Lord Rowbottom's suggestion, for 'tea and biscuits'.

Tony escorted them up to the sixth floor. He let them into the room.

Lord Rowbottom didn't waste any time. He removed his yellow tie and jacket. He kicked off his shoes and sat on the end of the bed. Amira turned her back to him at the far end of the room. She breathed deep and composed herself.

"Oh Amira, dear, I'm waiting for you."

Amira turned around with an artificial smile. She strolled across the carpet, pretending to be someone else. A persona. The high-class escort. She'd even given her a name: Deanna

Rowbottom could have Deanna, but he couldn't have Amira.

She'd hatched the plan the night before. A way of doing what was necessary, while insulating herself as much as possible from the act itself.

Amira unbuttoned Lord Rowbottom's shirt, slow and seductive. His fierce cologne invaded her nasal passages. She ignored it and planted a gentle kiss on his cheek.

Lord Rowbottom cracked a devious smile. "Come on," he said. "I can get that from my wife." He grabbed Amira by the arms and threw her face-first onto the bed. As she rose off the duvet, Rowbottom dragged her backwards on all fours. He pushed her dress up over her back. She heard the snap of leather as he ripped his belt from his trousers. She didn't want to look, but felt compelled to.

"You ever taken it up the bottom?" he asked her, down to a white vest, a pair of baggy pink boxer shorts, shiny black shoes and knee-high socks.

He snapped his belt in his hands and cracked Amira hard across the buttocks. Before she could stop herself, she kicked out in reply.

The kick didn't land.

"Like it rough, eh?" Lord Rowbottom said. "Two can play at that game. Come here."

Rowbottom kneeled on the bed behind her. He put a hand on her black silk knickers, attempting to yank them down. Amira spun around and slapped him across the face.

Rowbottom appeared to love it. He laughed and pushed her low on the bed. He took a handful of her hair and reached between her thighs.

Amira had lost all composure. Deanna was long gone. She dug her fingernails into Rowbottom's neck and drew blood.

He yelled in pain, reversing off the bed. "You demented bitch. There's a fucking limit."

The old man pulled on his pants, a trickle of blood down the side of his neck.

Tony stepped into the room. "Something wrong Lord Rowbottom?"

"Yes, something's wrong . . . With her."

"What did you do?" Tony said to Amira.

"Your whore dug her fucking claws in me, that's what. The wife will be all over this," Rowbottom pulled on his shirt, doing the buttons up uneven. "I'll need a ruddy tetanus shot now."

As Amira watched on from the bed, Tony attempted to calm his client down. "I'm sure we can arrange something—"

Rowbottom buckled up his belt. "Tell Pavel he can forget about the Silvertown motion."

Tony pulled a handful of tissues from a box on the

writing desk. He handed them to Rowbottom, who pressed them against the claw marks on his neck.

"Fucking amateurs," Rowbottom said, grabbing his jacket and tie.

As the old man stormed out of the room, Tony took out his phone. He called a number, pacing left and right.

"Boss, we've got a problem," he said. "No, it needs your attention. It's Rowbottom. I dunno what happened but he says the Silvertown deal is off."

Tony disappeared out of the room. As the door swung shut, Amira heard him calling Rowbottom's name along the corridor.

Amira felt a wave of relief, followed immediately by fear.

Chapter 51

I come around in a different room. A punch in the face my wake-up alarm. A clock on the wall telling me I've been out for the count around ten minutes.

No memory of how they put me to sleep, but my neck hurts like hell. My guess is a metal bar.

I take another knuckle sandwich in the left cheekbone. Two shaven apes in docker jackets taking turns to dish it out. So identikit, I can't even tell 'em apart.

Another guy watches on from the corner. Designer stubble and greying hair down to his shoulders. He's suave and trim in a navy suit and matching tie. A crisp white shirt. Everything tailored. He's a few cuts above a goon. Gotta be someone higher up. A general, or a captain at the very least.

He lets me take a couple more hits. Steps forward. Holds up a hand for the goons to stop.

I get my bearings. I'm strung up by the wrists, fixed to a steel rod that runs the length of the ceiling, tied tight with a length of rope. I'm on my tiptoes, so I hang and swing like an abattoir cow.

The room is nondescript. Solid steel walls and pipes. Not much else going on.

The man in the suit stands close to me. Speaks in a soft, Eastern European voice. And he speaks well, as if he's educated. "Hello," he says to me like I'm a little kid. "What's your name?"

"Popeye," I say. "What's yours?"

He smiles in the mouth, rather than the eyes. "My name's Pavel."

Pavel nods at the nearest goon. He feints to hit me in the face—drives a fist into my gut. I'm not ready and it winds the crap out of me.

I fight to regain my breath.

Pavel paces back and forth. Takes out his phone. "To be honest, I was just being polite. I know who you are, Charlie." He holds up the screen for me to see. They have me on CCTV, in the truck yard of Matheson Haulage.

It dawns on me they've got cameras on the ship, too.

I can't help laughing. "I walked right into this one, huh?" I spit out the blood off my tongue. "So Pavel, is this your operation, or is there an adult I can talk to?"

Pavel doesn't bite. He smiles instead. "Who are you working for Charlie?"

"Working for?"

Another punch. This time a right cross to the jaw. Now that one hurt.

"The less you talk, the longer we'll have to keep doing this." Pavel says.

I flex out my jaw. So Pavel thinks I work for someone. Probably the only reason I'm still alive.

I decide to play along. "What makes you think I'm working for anyone?"

Pavel inspects his nails. "Because only a fool would come after us alone."

Ah, so it's an *us*. That means there's someone above him.

"Who is it?" Pavel continues. "Eddie Prince?"

I cough and laugh at the same time. "Hardly."

"The police then? Major crimes? NCA? Interpol?"

"I don't work with fucking pigs," I say.

"Another outfit then," Pavel says, as if sure of it.

I pause a moment. One of the goons strides forward. Pavel halts him again with that magical hand of his.

"One name is all we need," Pavel says.

"And then what?"

"Then we cut you loose."

"Is that right?"

Pavel shrugs. "Well, maybe we follow you home to poppa. But don't worry, we'll be very discreet about it. They won't know it came from you."

I crease up. It hurts to laugh, but the guy amuses me.

"One name," Pavel says.

"Sorry mate, but you're a lousy interrogator. I would have broken out the—"

"Bucket and sponge?" Pavel prompts one of his goons to walk forward with a bucket and yellow sponge on a stick.

"I was gonna say blow torch, but yeah a damp sponge ought to do it."

Pavel looks down his nose at me as the other goon removes my boots and socks. "Pity you don't have the brain to go with that smart mouth of yours."

The goon pulls my t-shirt over and behind my head, exposing my chest.

Pavel tuts and shakes his head at the sight of my bruised body. "Look, Max. You should have aimed for the ribs. Too late now."

Pavel steps out of the way. The goon with the sponge on a stick dips it in the bucket. He pulls it out, sopping in water. It's freezing and makes me gasp.

"Cold?" Pavel asks. "How about we warm you up?" He motions to his goon, Max.

Max holds a streamlined black baton. His hands covered in a thick pair of red rubber gloves.

I brace myself, but nothing prepares you for frying alive.

He hits me with a bolt of electricity. Holds the baton to my skin while I convulse. Think of the worst cramp you've ever had and multiply it by a hundred. Then imagine it raging through your entire body—the worst of it in your chest.

The pain fades a little as they stop. Sweat pours out of me and my body tingles. And not in a fun way.

"Don't be silly now, Charlie. Tell me who you are. Southern? Northern?"

I don't say shit.

"European then?" he says.

I ignore the question. Just gotta—Christ, the second hit is worse. I almost black out.

Pavel continues with the questions. Max juices me a third time. I start to see things. Mandy in place of Max, smoking a cig and sticking me with the baton.

As I was gonna say, I've just gotta survive long enough

I've been in their shoes plenty of times. There's only so long you can question a guy using the same method. If they're any good at what they do, they'll change tactics, location, anything to get me to spill. And after all, they'll want me alive for at least another half an hour—just to be sure I'm not gonna talk.

As I gather my thoughts, a call interrupts the show. It's Pavel's phone. He answers it.

My vision blurs from beads of sweat dripping into my eyes. But I make out the time on the clock on the wall. We've been in here for a while. Can't be too long now.

Pavel babbles away in his mother tongue. I still don't know where the hell this lot are from. And I don't understand a bloody word of the nonsense pouring out of his mouth. But it sounds like I'm not the only one getting a grilling.

His face says it all. I know a call from the boss when I see one. Did a bigger cheese find out about the barracks? Pavel ends the call, shakes his head. Another call comes in the second he gets off the phone. He answers angry. Gets even angrier the longer he's on. "What did she do?" he says. "Keep him at the hotel until I get there . . . I don't know, use your brain you idiot!"

Pavel comes off the call. He talks to Max and the other goon. "Take him out on the boat. If he still doesn't talk, kill him and dump him."

As Pavel storms out of the room, I try to go somewhere else in my head. But all the escape hatches are locked. So all

I've got is unbearable cramping. I smell my own chest hair burning. It gets up my nose. Glad I didn't have the full fry-up at the greasy spoon or I'd have probably shat myself by now.

Max approaches with the baton. One more hit and I'm out.

Chapter 52

Woodington army barracks was a mess. A glorious mess of bodies, bullet holes and hard evidence. An entire Class A factory of it in the gym hall.

Not to mention a laptop full of schedules, stock reports and itineraries.

Cobb had not been exaggerating.

Detective Clarke stood with his back to the main building. He looked on as paramedics attended to the liberated refugees. Foil blankets wrapped around bodies. Steaming hot mugs in hands.

A white marquee had been set up away from the building. It served as both a temporary hospital and processing centre. The smell of smouldering ash filled the air. As fire crews and CSI criss-crossed in front of him, Clarke rested his behind against the warm bonnet of his Audi. He waited on the phone while Chief Superintendent Bridlington's PA put him through to his mobile.

"Clarke?" Bridlington said on the other end.

"Yes, sir."

"This had better be good. I'm at home with Diane."

"How is she, sir?"

"She's been better, What is it?"

"You know that breakthrough we've been waiting for?"

"Yes?"

"It's arrived. Oh boy, has it."

"Get to the point, Clarke."

"Right sir, well, looks like we've seized ourselves a ten million haul of coke. At least."

"Where?"

"Woodington barracks, out in the sticks."

"You sure it's connected to our case?"

"Oh, I'm certain, sir. We've got twenty or so slave labourers. And a laptop full of hard data."

Bridlington sounded surprised. "How did all that come about?"

"Anonymous tip, sir. Must have been a turf war. Eddie Prince is lying face-first in a cabbage field with a poker in his guts."

"Prince was part of this?"

"I assume so, sir. I've got an address for a second location. More of the same, I expect, along the Thames."

"Okay," Bridlington said, "I'll put in a request for surveillance."

"We need to act now, sir. We leave it much longer, they'll move on."

"You don't know that for certain, Clarke."

"I know these people, sir. One sniff of trouble and they shut up shop."

"Well whatever you think you know, I can't sign off a raid without prior surveillance."

"But sir—"

"But nothing. This is cigar time. It'll play well upstairs. I'm a happy fucking bunny. Wrap up there and file your report. We'll have a strategy meeting tomorrow, first thing."

Clarke pushed off the bonnet of the car. "With all due respect sir, they'll be in the wind by tonight and we'll be chasing our tails for another four years."

"Well unlike these savages, we've got procedures. Rome wasn't built in a day."

"Yeah but it was destroyed in no bloody time."

"You've had your orders, detective. Do your report. Go home and treat the missus to a chicken fucking balti. I'll see you tomorrow."

Clarke drew back his arm, ready to throw his phone across the tarmac. He resisted the urge, slumping back onto the bonnet of the car.

Morales appeared by his side. "Everything alright, guv?"

"Yeah, why?"

"Well we just won the lottery. And you look like you got the clap."

Clarke stood up. He walked around to the driver's side of the car and opened the door.

"Where are you going?" Morales asked.

"To see about the next location."

"They sign off the raid already?"

"Nope. I'm going it alone . . . Unless you fancy doing something incredibly stupid."

"Only if you tell me what's really going on," Morales said.

"You want in? Get in," Clarke said, ducking inside the car.

Morales hesitated as Clarke fired up the engine. "Oh, what the hell," she said, opening the passenger door.

Chapter 53

Can't breathe.

Can't fucking breathe.

The cold. The current. I wasn't ready.

They drag me up. The wind hits me and stings my skin.

I cough and splutter, filthy water running off me onto the deck.

They ask me again. I shake my head. Shiver on aching knees. Rough wooden boards digging in.

They dunk me back under. I fight to get out but there's two of 'em manhandling me, my hands tied behind my back.

Waves smash into my upper body as my head hangs beneath the surface. They hold me under for longer as the boat drags me sideways through the Thames.

The boat is cruising, but under the water, it feels like a hundred miles an hour. They haul me out one more time. I take a punch in a kidney. Another in the side of the neck. My feet are blocks of ice. I can't feel my toes.

We're out in the choppier end of the river. A lesser-travelled part where no one is around to watch. The surrounding docks and railway bridges appear tiny on the shore. The heart of the city a distant, hazy shadow behind a veil of smog.

They ask me again who I'm working for. I shake my head some more. Laugh at 'em. Tell 'em where to shove it. Max and his hairy lookalike wrestle me over the side again and dunk me back in.

My eyes are open as they force my head underneath. All I see is a thick murk and a line of bubbles escaping as I fight to hold in the oxygen.

They pull me up. Let me drop to my knees a fifth time, gasping for air.

The questions have stopped, which means the time is approaching.

The boat is small and old. Open at the back, shielded at the front by a windscreen and roof.

A third guy stands at the wheel. Dressed like the other two, but small and skinny. A blonde mullet, an ear ring and a worn-out face.

"Stop it here," Max yells over the chug and diesel stench of the engine.

The boat slows down. I stare straight ahead at the cracked black paint on the edge of the deck. I shake the water out of my ears so I can hear better. Jet a line of water out of my nose.

Hands, head, feet, the whole lot red raw.

I look around me and see a brown sack in the corner, with a rusty chain, a padlock and two large concrete bricks.

"Last chance to talk," Max says, pulling out a handgun.

He taps the side of my head with the long silencer barrel.

I stay quiet. Get ready. There's *always* a window.

The boat comes to a stop and bobs up and down in the water.

If they've got any brains about 'em, they'll hold me over the side while they put a bullet through my skull. That way you don't have to clean any fleshy bits off the deck. Or, they'll bag my head up first so the inside catches the splatter.

They choose the second option. While Max fiddles with his gun, the other pulls a clear plastic bag from his coat pocket.

Their hands are off me for a few seconds.

That's the window.

I drive up off my feet and knees. I stagger the few steps to the side of the boat. Max shoots, but it's too late, I'm diving head-first into the water. The freezing temperature shocks me to the core.

Bullets follow me in, each with a snaking white tail. I spin around with my eyes open. I kick my way below the boat and tread water underneath. As more bullets zip into the river, I tuck my knees to my chest and bring my hands under my feet. I bring 'em around my front and work my way across the belly of the boat to the opposite side.

I'm running out of breath, fast. Unbearable pressure building in my chest and throat.

No choice but to break out onto the surface. I stay tight to the hull. Quiet gasps of air, surviving on adrenaline.

I hear the men shouting at each other. More silencer rounds fired into the water. They soon give up.

"Forget it," I hear the driver of the boat say. "If the bullets didn't get him, the cold soon will. He's either dead or drowning by now."

"Fine," Max says. "Let's go back. I need a shit anyway."

"You dirty fucker," his goon pal says.

"What?" Max says. *"I do."*

The engine splutters into life and the boat turns to the left. The upper side of the hull is lined by small black tyres cut in half. They're strung together by rope, acting as bumpers. I grab a length of the rope and stay low, out of sight.

The boat turns around and picks up speed. I bounce through the chop, getting a face full of white water. I hang on and cough the stuff out. Blink it out of my eyes. I slap hard off the surface, but I pull one leg up out of the river. I get a slippery foothold on one of the rubber bumpers and pull myself out of the worst of it. I get a grip of the side of the boat and peep over the edge. Max and his pal are stood towards the bow, behind the driver.

While their backs are turned, I haul my weight up and onto the deck. The chug, chop and wind obliterate the heavy, wet slap I make as I hit the wood. With the docks growing bigger and the city skyline getting closer, I pick up one of the concrete bricks they brought with 'em to weigh down my body.

I stagger forward. Max happens to turn his head. He sees me dripping head to toe, angry as hell. He draws his gun from his holster.

I hurl the concrete brick. It hits him with a *thunk* on the forehead.

He wobbles, eyes rolling white and blood streaming from his

head. He trips over the edge of the boat and falls in backwards, taking his gun with him. As Max's mate reacts, I hit him with closed fists, once, twice . . . three times knocks him overboard.

I turn to the driver. He panics, grabs a life ring hanging beneath the wheel and jumps over the side. I use my teeth to prise one of the goon's incisors from between my knuckles. I spit it out.

As the boat bounces up and down, the wheel spins one way and the other.

I return to the back of the boat and pick up the chain. I carry it to the front, grab the wheel and steady the boat out. I spot Cristina in the distance. I head straight for her, roping the chain around the wheel. I use hands, teeth, feet, anything I can to fix it firm.

I tie it off on a steel strut supporting the roof, then push the throttle all the way forward.

The boat bounces high off the water. I stagger to the back of the boat.

When they were torturing me, I spotted a red plastic can of emergency petrol. There's also a green box with a flare inside. I unscrew the cap off the petrol.

I back-pedal with the can, pouring a line of petrol the length of the deck. I empty the last of the stuff over the windscreen as Cristina's sea-stained blue hull looms large.

We must be doing thirty knots by now, so I won't have long to pull this off. I remove the top off the flare with my teeth. I hold the striking surface outwards from my mouth and hold up the end of the flare where it ignites.

Kids, definitely don't do this at home.

Chapter 54

I strike the top of the flare across the rough surface of the cap. It takes three attempts before it lights.

It sparks orange and red. I nearly take my eyebrows off before I can pull it away from my face. I spit out the cap, feeling the heat coming off the flare. A cloud of red smoke streams out behind me, the smell of sulphur and petrol mixing in with diesel fumes.

I wait . . . I wait . . . I toss it onto the deck. It rolls in the petrol. It catches. A blue and orange flame shooting from stern to bow.

I jump and hit the water like a bouncing bomb. I spin in a ball beneath the surface. Amazing how similar it feels to jumping from a moving car.

I bob up in time to see the boat ablaze, torpedoing into the side of the ship. There's a huge explosion. The boat breaks in two and rips a hole in the hull of the ship.

Rather than enjoy the view, I'm already kicking to dry land. I'm a strong swimmer and used to the ice cold river by now. I wriggle through the water as fast as a man can with both hands bound at the wrists.

I head straight for an iron ladder attached to the dock wall. It's red with surface rust. I grab hold of the third rung up. I lift my lower half out of the water and get a foothold on the bottom rung. I push off my feet and catch hold of the next rung up.

Like a caterpillar climbing a tree, I contort my way to the top. I roll onto the dock. I struggle to my feet and run alongside the ship. One of Pavel's men is already onto me. He stands on the deck, spraying the dock with machine gun fire.

I evade the bullets and stoop low, tackling a goon fleeing the ship. I hit him with both hands and get his automatic weapon. I break his jaw with the butt, turn and fire back at the man on the deck of the ship.

I miss by a mile: a rubbish shot with my hands tied up. As the guy reloads, I bound up the steps onto the deck. I dart in through the entrance to the body of the ship. I've gotta get my hands out of these ties.

I look around me and see a jagged edge of metal where a rusty panel has come free of a few bolts. A small mercy in an unforgiving world.

I drop the weapon and hook both wrists over the sharp edge. I start rubbing like crazy, back and forth, an alarm going off on board the ship: a deep whop-whop.

I'm halfway through the plastic tie already. Skin peeling off the insides of my wrists. But there's a problem.

A big one.

A big, hairy forearm around my neck. A hand on the back of my head for leverage. I rub even faster.

Looks like they sent the biggest piece of shit on board to put me out of their misery.

Either he's gonna snap my neck or crush my windpipe—whichever comes first. I keep rubbing, drawing blood from my own skin. Threatening to slice open an artery. The friction burning. I don't care. Gotta get out of these ties.

Yes! They snap. I reach behind me. Feel a face full of wiry hair. A bald head. A pair of eyeballs. My thumbs going in, pressing hard.

He screams in my ear. Lets me go and backs off blind. He's a pale guy with a mess of a ginger beard and a flabby frame busting out of a tight white t-shirt.

As he wanders back into me, I grab a metal beam overhead and swing both feet towards him.

I have visions of kicking him down the stairs behind him, but he catches me by the soggy ankles of my jeans. He rips me off the beam and slams me down on my back.

I bounce like a ball off a steel mesh flooring. I groan and roll, but no time to pick myself up. The bastard's on top of me, pinning me down. A rather large knife pulled from a sheath on his belt.

He angles the point of the blade towards my face. I catch hold of his stabbing hand and stop the momentum. He wraps his other hand around mine and leans all his weight into it. I push back with everything I have, but he's got the leverage.

At six-seven and twenty-odd stone—that's a lot of leverage. And he's starting to win the war. I've got nothing left. I try and roll him off, but no joy. He inches the blade towards my right eyeball, the knife getting closer, closer . . .

Chapter 55

The blade is all set to puncture my retina. Nothing but a blur.

I wait for the blinding pain. Death to follow soon after.

But a shot rings out.

I find some extra strength. A lot of it. I push back and realise the guy's arms have gone limp. He's wearing a bullet hole between the eyes, blood streaming down his face, into his beard.

Knife still in hands, he flops sideways onto the mesh floor.

I look up and see a pair of long legs standing over me. A lanky bastard in a grey suit.

Detective Clarke holsters his weapon.

"You took your bloody time," I say.

Clarke extends a hand. He helps me to my feet.

"You bring the cavalry?" I ask.

"If by cavalry, you mean . . . "Clarke looks behind him. Detective Morales appears. Low on breath with a weapon of her own held tight in both hands.

"Thought detectives weren't supposed to carry guns."

"Technically, we're not," Clarke says. "But I'm not about to die on a technicality."

I laugh and rub my neck. "You're gonna get in some serious shit for this."

Clarke looks around him. "We're not in it already?"

There's a rumbling in the belly of the ship. A deep explosion from the starboard side. We move over to the guard rail running along the far right of the deck. I cough on a rising funnel of acrid black smoke.

The ship groans and rocks a foot to the right. Huge swathes of river water rush in through a gaping hole in the hull.

The boat I used as a missile is a flaming wreck. It detaches from the ship and slips beneath the water.

"Charlie," Detective Clarke says. "What the hell did you do?"

"It was meant to be a distraction," I say.

"It's distracting alright," says Morales.

"Look, I've had a tough afternoon."

"Tell me about it later," Clarke says. "We've got to get off here."

"We can't," I say. "They're keeping women on the ship."

"They'll find their own way out," says Morales.

"They're drugged up to their eyeballs. Half of 'em can't even move."

"Where?" Clarke asks.

I point between my feet.

"You've gotta be kidding," he says.

I shrug and start towards the stairs leading below deck. Clarke and Morales stand looking at each other. "Well?" I say, picking up the discarded machine gun.

Morales curses under her breath. Clarke shakes his head, but they follow me down into the bowels of the ship.

* * *

Lights blinking. Wiring sparking. We meet with resistance along the way. Automatic rounds from the remaining crew abandoning ship.

We flatten out inside doorways and return fire. Morales is a good shot. Clarke less so, but I make up for it with a spray of machine gun fire. Between us, we dispatch the remaining crew.

We drop down the second staircase. The brown, oily river creeping in around the bottom step. My feet are still thawing out, but here we go again. I jump in and run ahead of the detectives, trying to remember the way to the main cargo hold.

The further we head towards the bow, the higher the water rises around our ankles.

Clarke is on his phone. "Shit," he says. "Can't get a signal."

"There's no time anyway," I say, splashing shin-high through the freezing water. "Follow me."

Coming the other way, I see Nabil. He spots me and turns to run. I speed up after him. He trips and falls into the water. I pull him up by his collar.

I wave Clarke and Morales onwards. "The women are straight ahead. I'll catch you up."

Clarke and Morales pass me by, cursing the cold water—suit trousers soaked and ruined.

I shove Nabil against the nearest wall. "Where's Amira?"

"Who?"

"The girl I wanted to see."

"Are you crazy?" he says in a panic. "The ship is sinking."

"Then talk, or we're both going down with this thing."

The ship lurches again, as if to make my point.

"Shit, okay," Nabil says. "She's at the Mercia."

"The where?"

"It's a hotel. Pavel's using her as an escort. High-class fuck."

"Which room?"

"Let me go," Nabil says. "I can't swim."

"Which room?"

"Six-twelve."

I let go of the scumbag. He turns and runs off towards freedom. I fire an automatic round in his back. He collapses, face flat and arms out in the water.

"Oops," I say.

I catch up to Clarke and Morales at the doorway to the cargo hold. A few of the girls are out of their beds. Disoriented. Panicking. Morales beckons them towards her as me and Clarke wade deeper into the hold.

I take the lefthand row, Clarke the other. We throw the curtains open on all the cubicles, the ship listing to the right.

I unhook the first woman from her morphine drip. She's just a girl, weak as wilted lettuce. I pull her over one shoulder and carry her out of the cubicle. There's another woman on my row, a couple of beds down. She's a little more awake. A plump African girl screaming at me. Confused out of her mind, like she's woken up in the middle of a nightmare.

"Come on," I say, waving her out of her bed. "We've gotta go."

The ship shudders. She shakes her head and cries. Frozen in fear. The water rising around the legs of the bed. Smoke invading the cargo hold.

"It's okay, I'm here to help," I say, taking her by the arm.

She shakes and slaps me off, not having any of it.

I look along the hold and see Detective Clarke. He fireman-carries a young woman away. Another staggers through the water alongside him.

I turn to the remaining woman. She's going bananas, but I'm not leaving her. So I pop her in the cheek. A tap with my fist that puts her out cold. I scoop her off the bed under one arm. I carry the two women out, the water making it heavy going. Smoke making it hard to see.

I cough my lungs out, following Clarke and Morales towards the stairs. Now that the goons are long gone, I let the rifle slip off the end of my shoulder.

We wade through the icy water, fire raging inside a few of the rooms along the corridor. We make it to the stairs in the nick of time. The water rises fast behind us as the ship continues to tilt to the right.

"Hurry up," I shout ahead of me as we lumber up the stairs.

"What do you think I'm doing?" Clarke shouts back.

As we struggle up the next set of stairs, two dock workers

in high-vis orange appear. One of them pulls the girl off Clarke's shoulder. Another grabs the woman under my arm.

Morales herds the walking wounded out onto the deck. I reach the top, but hear a scream. A large swell forms around the bottom of the stairs, carrying a young woman with it. The same young woman Pavel used to trick me, earlier in the day.

"Come on!" Clarke shouts at me. "What are you waiting for?"

"We left one behind," I say, flopping the girl on my shoulder onto the top of the steps. "Get out of here."

Clarke drags the unconscious woman out by the armpits. I look below and see the remaining girl flapping around. She's hit by another wave and sucked underneath. I vault over the side of the rail and plunge feet first into the swirl.

Chapter 56

Amira paced the carpet. She clutched a brass candlestick holder, taken from one of the deep window sills of the room. It weighed heavy, its edges sharp

She heard voices outside the door. She backed up close to the wall, heels kicked off and bare feet ready to run. She heard the lock in the door. Saw the door knob turn.

It would be her one and only chance. As the door opened, she swung the candlestick holder high.

She connected with her target, but only a glancing blow. Tony raised a forearm in time to deflect the base of the brass holder away from his temple. In the same move, he snatched the weapon from Amira's hands.

He pushed her deeper into the room and laughed to himself. "Silly bitch."

Pavel wasn't amused. He strode up to Amira with thunder in his eyes. He shoved her onto the end of the bed.

Amira scrambled away. Pavel stepped onto the bed and stood over her. He dropped to his knees, straddling her waist. He looked over his shoulder.

Tony took the hint, closing and locking the door behind him.

Pavel pinned Amira down by the throat. "I've spent the last hour in the lobby, trying to make peace with Rowbottom. Have you any fucking idea how much you've cost us?"

Amira glanced around her for another weapon. Nothing but a plastic telephone to her right, out of reach on a bedside table.

"Well?" Pavel said.

Amira shook her head as best she could.

"Take a guess."

"A thousand?" she said, choking.

"Millions," Pavel said. "The old man was going to push through a land deal. But thanks to you, it's gone. I treat you like a fucking queen and this is how you repay me?"

If Amira wasn't struggling to breathe, she would have laughed. *Repay him?* The only way to repay Pavel was a bullet to the brain.

He let go of her throat and breathed deep, as if talking himself down from murder. He pushed his hair from his face and reversed off the bed. He straightened his jacket and calmed his voice. "You want out of here? Fine."

Amira sat up, rubbing her throat. "You'll let me leave?"

Pavel straightened his tie. "If you're not going to service our clients, all you are is an expense. Put your shoes on."

Pavel shouted Tony into the room. "Tell Anton to bring the car around front."

Amira slid off the bed and stepped into her heels.

Chapter 57

Eyes open, I see the white gown of the girl, billowing out under the water. I swim after her, catch hold of her and pull her backwards.

We surface together. I'm relieved to hear her screaming and yelling. We ride the rising water up to the top of the stairs. I plant a foot on the step and drag the girl out onto the deck. A fire blazes towards the bow. The floor leans at a forty degree angle. I climb up the slope, pushing the girl on. I look over the edge: Clarke and Morales stand at a safe distance with the other girls and those dock workers.

Squad cars and fire engines rush wailing onto the scene.

I scoop the girl up in one arm, not giving her any say. The stairs are out as they no longer reach the dock wall. The port-side hull leans away from shore.

I swing my legs over the edge of the ship and slide under the guard rail running along the deck. The girl shakes her head. I push off regardless.

I slide arse-first along the exposed hull. Lucky for us it's dirty. The muck and rust slows the ride. The girl screams anyway. We hit the dock in a heap. But we're both okay. I drag the girl onto her feet and look up at the ship. It's sinking fast, the starboard side submerged in the Thames.

"Well there goes the next lot of evidence," Clarke says to me, breathing heavy, his face black with soot.

"You moaning bastard," I say, wandering off.

"Where are you going?" Morales asks, shivering wet.

"Gotta take care of something," I say, breaking into a jog.

"Cobb!" Clarke shouts. "Cobb! Get back here!"

I ignore the guy and run as fast as my frozen bones will let me. I'm parked a hundred yards and a couple of streets away. I find a big yellow clamp on the front driver's wheel.

Well, at least I've got weapons in the boot. I dig a hand inside my pocket. The key fob comes out sopping wet. Doesn't work. I throw it away and start running.

I hit the main road and flag down a black cab. The driver's a chubby forty-something in a red polo shirt.

I talk to him through the window. "How far's the Mercia from here?"

"Couple of minutes," he says. "At the top of this road and then right."

"Great," I say, "That's where we're going."

"You're not getting in my cab like that, mate."

"Oh come on pal, it's an emergency."

"Not my problem," he says, pulling away.

I give him a mouthful and start running. I see a large white van pulling out onto the road behind me. I wait for it to pass by and jump on the back. I stand on the rear bumper and ride it all the way up the road. I hop off as it makes a right turn into a busy street full of shops and bars. The momentum sees me run across the road in front of beeping, braking traffic.

I dodge my way through and onto the pavement. I see the Mercia Hotel on the left. A plush, high-rise glass building with blue tinted windows. It sits behind a fountain and a stretch of perfectly cut grass.

I see a car pulling up out front. A shiny silver Mercedes saloon. A big guy with a greased-back pony tail shoving a woman in a posh frock into the backseat.

Amira.

Pavel, too, climbing in beside her.

The big guy gets in the front and the car pulls out onto the road.

I look around. Spot a black cab parking up in its place. I run towards it. The driver gets out. The same joker who refused me a ride. He's round the back of the cab, helping a couple with their luggage. I run straight past 'em and jump in behind the wheel. I take off. Leave the cab driver bawling and flapping in the rearview.

I'm soon up to speed and settle into a thirty mile-an-hour cruise. The silver Mercedes is a few cars up ahead. It indicates right and makes a turn. I tail the car through a series of swanky streets.

The Mercedes makes a left turn and I follow at a safe distance behind. There are no cars between us now and the driver of the Merc won't look twice at a following cab. All I have to do is track 'em to wherever they're going.

We stop at a set of lights. They turn green. We set off.

Then some arsehole comes out of a side street in a yellow Porsche. He cuts between me and the Merc.

Pavel's driver speeds up to make a right turn through a gap in traffic. By the time the Porsche zooms off ahead, I'm blocked from making the same turn by cars coming the other way. I sit with the indicator on, waiting for a gap. There isn't one. So I make one, accelerating across a double-decker London bus.

The cab is an inch from being wiped out.

But I make it into a quiet road. It's lined by tall, stone buildings. Traditional gaffes behind black, wrought iron bars. I give it beans up the road, playing catch up. I slam on at a T-junction and look both ways. The Mercedes is gone.

Chapter 58

Anton, Pavel's driver, steered the Mercedes down a ramp off a quiet London street. The headlights clicked on as they rolled into an underground car park. They cruised past Bentleys, BMWs and a red Ferrari.

Amira tensed up on the backseat of the car. The journey had taken place in icy silence. She knew any hope that Pavel would release her was wishful thinking. She wondered what was in store next.

Anton parked the Mercedes in a space with no cars either side. Tony hauled his giant frame out of the passenger seat with a wheeze. He threw his door shut and opened the rear door for Pavel.

Pavel got out. Amira craned her neck to see him walk around the back of the car. He opened her door. Amira hesitated.

"Come on," Pavel said, checking his watch. "We haven't got long."

"Until what?" Amira asked.

"You can either get out, or Tony will drag you out," Pavel said.

Amira swung both feet out onto the car park floor. She rose out of the Mercedes and walked towards the elevator, Pavel gripping her forearm tight, the air chilly. They rode up three floors before the doors slid open.

Pavel yanked Amira out of the elevator, across a white marble floor. Large gold vases stood against walls, holding tall arrangements of bamboo.

Amira thought it expensively tasteless. "When are you going to let me go?" she asked, hoping Pavel would get frustrated with her. Give her the truth.

But Pavel stared straight ahead. Dead in the eyes, as if she no longer existed.

They moved along a clean white corridor, Tony's rubber soles squeaking over the floor. Pavel's and her own clapping in chorus.

They came to a reception area.

The young woman behind the desk was rake-thin with pinned-up red hair. She picked up a receiver on a phone behind the counter top. "Your guests have arrived," she said, in a plum accent. She put down the phone and smiled at Pavel. "They're ready for you. Meeting Room Four." The receptionist pointed to her right, along another corridor. As they passed by, her smile fell and her freckled nose wrinkled at the sight of Amira.

A bearded man in tweed walked by with a stethoscope around his neck. A nurse in a crisp white uniform stepped out of a doorway and shuffled off ahead. Amira thought back to the doctor who had visited her in the hotel room. At the time, she thought the blood and urine tests were to check she was free of infection. Now she wasn't so sure.

As they arrived at Meeting Room Four, she wondered what it could all mean.

The two men guarding the door didn't bode well. They resembled secret service agents, or Italian mafia. With sunglasses and complexions from a warmer climate.

They stepped aside. Tony opened the door. Pavel straightened his suit and tie. He put a hand on the small of Amira's back and guided her into the room.

Two men sat in cream leather swing chairs to the far right of a polished walnut table dominating the room. One wore a black suit and a matching roll neck sweater underneath. He was a stocky man with brown hair, slicked back and grey at the temples. His skin tanned and sun-spotted. A pair of large, brown-tinted glasses concealed his eyes from view. A well-fed midriff hung off his frame.

The man rested an arm on a dark, folded raincoat draped on the chair to his left. He turned to look at Amira

"Mr Grezda," Pavel said. "Forgive the intrusion."

"Is this the one?" the other man at the table asked. He was bald and appeared tall, even sitting down. And he wore a navy police uniform buttoned up and adorned with stripes on each arm.

Pavel guided Amira towards the men. "This is her," he said. "As you can see, she's young and in perfect health."

"You have her bloods?" the policeman asked.

"She's clean as a . . . How do you say here?" Pavel asked.

"A whistle," the police officer said.

"Yes, that's it."

Grezda looked at the officer. "Well, what do you think?" He spoke in an accent similar to Pavel's, only worn by time and the cigars he smelled of.

"An excellent candidate," the policeman said. "How soon can we do this? My wife's condition—"

"We can proceed right away," Grezda said, waving a calming hand.

The policeman took out his phone and began to text. "I'll let Diane's carer know. I'll have a car pick them up." He looked up from his phone. "Thank you, Edgar."

"You've been a good friend to us," Grezda said, before hesitating. "And I hate to ask at a time like this, but—"

"Sure, what is it?" the officer said, distracted.

As Grezda waved Pavel away, he turned to talk to the policeman. "We're experiencing some resistance from a man called Rowbottom. He might need a little persuasion . . ."

Amira found herself shoved out into the corridor.

"What's going on?" she asked Pavel. "What are you all talking about?"

"Please be quiet, dear," Pavel said as they walked to another elevator. "I'm sick of your whining."

Amira shook off his grip. She waited for Tony to choose a floor. They were going up a level. As the doors began to close, she darted out through the gap.

She turned to see the doors close behind her. The elevator going up, with Pavel and Tony stuck inside. She kicked off her heels and bolted back along the corridor. She pushed her away through a pair of nurses and skidded into reception.

The receptionist had seen Amira coming. She stepped

out from behind her desk. "Hey, where are you—"

Amira knocked her to the floor. She ran onwards and found the elevator that had brought her up from the car park. She pushed the button, but it was taking too long. She saw a door to a set of stairs to her right. She took off through the door, scrambling down the stairs, a steadying hand on the railing.

Each floor was marked by a number. First came two, then one. The next would be the ground floor.

But there was a man coming the other way, on his phone. "No sign of her. I'm taking the stairs." He looked up and saw Amira. It was Anton, with his gelled black hair and an angular face. "Wait, I've got her!"

Amira spun and ran back up the stairs, the energy draining from her legs. Anton yelled for her to stop.

She didn't.

Instead, she was counting the floors to the top, thinking there might be another way out. Thinking she could lose them on one of the higher floors. Then double back and exit the building.

She ran up past the second floor, rounded the landing and ran for the third.

There stood Pavel.

And Tony, up above on the fourth.

Anton catching up fast behind.

Amira looked over the bannister. Saw a drop to the basement floor. There was space enough between flights of stairs. The railings supporting the bannister had horizontal struts halfway up. She stepped on a strut and leaned out over the bannister.

All she had to do was let go. Her own weight and momentum would take her the rest of the way.

"No!" Pavel yelled, his cries echoing throughout the stairwell. A hand outstretched towards her.

Amira closed her eyes and prayed rapidly under her breath. She got ready to let go.

Chapter 59

I drive around, looking for the Merc.

There's no sign. It can't have gone that far. Must have got off the street somehow. I double back along the road I lost it down. I pull up outside a tall, stone building. A fancy-looking place with a sign outside that says *Chesterton Private Clinic*. There's a metal shutter to the right of the building. It opens. A dark-blue Bentley Continental emerges onto the street.

I take a chance, playing a hunch. I steer the cab down the ramp and cut underneath the shutter before it closes. I find myself in an underground car park full of gleaming supercars. I make a left turn and cruise along a row. There, at the end of the row, I see the Merc. At least, I think it's the one. I drive past and turn right and right again onto the next row. I park up and turn off the engine. I get out and jog between cars, staying low. The smooth car park floor is cool on my bare feet. I slide between a Lambo and a Range Rover, both smelling of fresh wax.

I approach the Mercedes.

It's empty.

I look across the car park and see a lift at the far end. I run over to it and push the button. It comes down from an upper level.

It opens up.

There's a man inside with black gelled hair. He's on the phone. He drops it when he sees me. Swings a fist. I connect first, knocking him flat on his back.

I push the button for the ground floor and find the guy's wallet. His driver's licence says *Anton Glick*. I bet any money that he's the driver.

The lift hits the ground floor and the doors open to a marble foyer with a security guard behind a desk. I jab the button fast to close the doors. They slide shut before the guard can look up from his paper. I press for the first. The doors open. I step out into a tall, wide corridor. More bloody marble. There's money in this place, alright.

I wander round but don't find anything other than offices. The clinic must be further up. I get back in the lift and choose the fourth floor out of six. Before long, I'm stepping out into a white corridor. No more marble. This is more like a hospital. The look, the smell, the vibe.

I set off along the corridor. Walking slow. Staying tight to the wall, in case I need to duck into a room and hide.

A surgeon barges through a set of swinging doors in blue scrubs. I peer inside one of the windows. See a man on an operating table.

He's African. Skinny. Out for the count under a green surgical sheet. Another doctor in scrubs places a kidney in a stainless steel dish.

I find another room. A ward. Three beds with women hooked up to drips, as if recovering from surgeries of their own.

I move on, but hear two people talking. Nurses coming round the corner.

Can't let anyone see me like this. They'll raise the alarm.

So I push into a room. It's dark, but the lights flicker on automatically. I back up and bump up against something hard and metal. The edge of a gurney. A blue-skinned big toe sticking out from under a light-blue sheet. I turn and see three gurneys in a row. Each with a body underneath. I pull the top ends of the sheets away.

I take a step back.

Shit.

They're just kids.

Two teenage girls and a young boy.

They look like migrants to me. Dark-skinned and underfed.

I've seen some stuff in my time, but this . . . You can blow a shotgun hole in a goon's face. Chop a couple of fingers off a dealer. But you don't cut out people's organs—kidneys, lungs, the little boy's eyes.

Can't think what I'd do if this was my Cassie . . . And suddenly, it all connects. The bodies in the mortuary. The illegal clinics Clarke was talking about. Bodies buried in the foundations under new building projects. The building site development owned by VX Holdings, Prince's company.

And Eddie Prince working for a slice of the pie for Pavel and his mates.

People smuggling. Slave labour. Prostitution. And now organ harvesting. All this time I thought I was moving further up the chain. When all I've really been doing is dropping deeper into hell.

And they've brought Amira here.

Chapter 60

She could have screamed.

Her body wouldn't move. Her hand wouldn't let go of the bannister. Her foot wouldn't push off the strut. And before she could step down off the railing, Anton was there to wrap his arms around her waist. He pulled her back from the bannister and carried her fighting and kicking up to the third floor. Without a word, Pavel grabbed a handful of Amira's hair and dragged her up the stairs to the fourth. He pushed her into the arms of Tony, who manhandled her onto the fifth, as if she was something to be passed around. Tony shoved her through the stairwell door and back into the clinic.

This floor was different. No more meeting rooms. No more marble. All white and clean. At least on the surface.

Amira soon found herself in a private room. A hard-faced blonde nurse with tattoos walked in with a porter pushing a bed on wheels.

"Help me get her clothes off," the nurse said.

Amira resisted the attentions of Tony, but the nurse was

already undoing the zip on the back of her dress. Amira fought harder, but nurse, porter and Tony had her down on the bed between them—her underwear removed. The nurse tied a white smock loose around her back.

Tony and the porter forced her legs onto the bed. They pinned her down flat and motionless on top of the sheets.

As the nurse inserted a drip into the back of her hand, Pavel talked into his phone. He was angry, pacing to and fro. *"What do you mean, Cristina's gone? How?"*

Amira wanted to tear the drip from the back of her hand. But it was taped tight to her skin. And Tony was too strong. She felt the cold flow of water creeping up her forearm.

"No," Pavel said, still on the call. "Go through the usual channels. Have the women sent back... *To where?* To Hungary, Romania, I don't care, just get rid of them... In fact, get them to Romania. Dimi will know what to do with them."

As Amira listened to Pavel's conversation, the nurse forced a mask over her head, the porter holding her still at the temples. She felt a current of air coming in through the mask, invading her nose and mouth. She was pretty sure it wasn't oxygen. She attempted to breath slow and shallow.

"No, no, no," Pavel continued. "We've got a man who can make the barracks go away." Pavel paused on the phone. "No, I can't. I'm at the clinic... Sick wife. Wants to shortcut the waiting list."

With the nurse and Tony holding Amira down, the porter got behind the bed. Together, they wheeled her out into the corridor.

Pavel walked close behind. "Fine, just let me know when it's done. The old man's here and he'll want answers."

It was a short trip along the corridor. The porter pushed the end of the bed through a set of swinging double doors. They opened into a circular theatre with an operating table in the centre. Amira glanced at the array of gleaming tools next to the table. A variety of scalpels and what appeared to be a small, circular bone saw.

She would have hyperventilated, had the gas from the mask not been flooding her mind and body.

She attempted to lift her arms. To remove the mask. They were heavy as lead, the anaesthetic taking effect.

The porter wheeled the bed to the right of the operating table and parked it against a wall.

"The surgical team are prepping," the nurse said to Tony. "They'll be here soon."

The nurse and porter left the operating room, leaving Pavel and Tony alone with Amira.

Pavel tucked his phone away in his jacket. "Give us five minutes alone," he said to Tony.

Tony nodded. "I'll be outside."

Pavel strolled over to the bed, leaned over Amira and smiled. "Can you see now, I was trying to help you? You should have helped me. I would have liked things to have gone differently. But everyone must have a use."

For once, Amira agreed with Pavel. She wished she'd played along at the hotel. She wished she'd taken her own life, rather than have Pavel and his people profit from it.

Pavel ran his fingers through the hair over her forehead.

"There's nothing to be concerned about, dear. The doctor's going to cut out your heart and give it to someone else, that's all."

Amira found her eyesight splitting and blurring. She saw two of Pavel.

She didn't feel his lips pressing against her forehead, or her neck. Or the hand pushing her gown up her legs. His hand creeping up the inside of her right thigh. "Can't resist me now, can you?" Pavel said, climbing onto the bed. He slipped his belt out from its loops. "Don't worry. You won't feel a thing."

Amira began a silent prayer. For mercy. Revenge. Divine intervention.

Not expecting, but hoping.

But in the depths of her despair, she saw the doors to the operating room fly open. A white cloud of smoke appearing in the room.

A figure materialised in the cloud. Skin like ash and eyes like fire.

When she was young, Amira's father had told her stories of jinn, spirit creatures made of smoke. If you were bad, he'd said, the evil jinn would appear out of thin air and snatch your soul.

Pavel paused with his hands on his buckle. He glanced over his shoulder. The creature strode out of the smoke. Barefoot and dressed in rags.

The jinn had come to claim a soul.

Chapter 61

I catch sight of myself in a tinted window. A sopping wet cindered mess. Beaten up and worn out with nerve endings still screaming from the interrogation.

It's a weird feeling. Like I'm burning and freezing at the same time. I've managed to move through the fourth floor of the clinic unseen. The corridor leads to a dead end ahead, but there's a left turn. I stay tight to the wall. Peer around it. See the same big fella I saw getting into the Mercedes. The one in the bulky black suit with the jet-black hair in a ponytail. He stands in front of a pair of blue doors with porthole windows. It says *Theatre 3* above the doors. A pair of surgeons in full scrubs and masks hurry towards the room. He waves them away. Tells them to give it five minutes.

They shake their heads. Throw out their arms and complain. The guy doesn't blink. They shuffle off back from where they came. I edge out slow, along the corridor. He hasn't seen me yet, so I steal a small red fire extinguisher off the wall. I hold it behind my back and pull the pin from the handle.

Now he sees me. Wrinkles his brow. Waves me away.

"You," he says. "Turn around."

I keep walking.

"Turn around," he says, stepping away from the doors.

I keep walking. I'm close now.

He gets anxious. Shows me the butt of his pistol. "Look buddy, it's fucking-off time, yeah?"

I whip the extinguisher out from behind my back. I pull the trigger and blast the guy in the face. I smash him in the skull with the end. A metallic *bong* later, he's on the floor. White vapour everywhere. I step over the man's foam-covered body. Hear another man's voice inside the operating room. I'd know that voice anywhere. It's Pavel. And I hear him say Amira's name.

I drop the extinguisher and barge through the doors.

Chapter 62

I burst in through the doors. A white cloud from the extinguisher follows me in. It wisps away as I get my bearings.

The room is big and round. An operating table with a tray of tools on a stand next to it. There's a bright cluster of lights over the table. Everything is spotless and the room smells of detergent.

I see a hospital bed to my right. Amira lying on top, with Pavel kneeling over her, about to take his pants off. He freezes in surprise.

I stride up to the bed.

One hand on his belt, the other on his left ankle, I drag him off her and throw him across the room.

He bounces and rolls.

Amira lies motionless on the bed in a surgical gown. I hurry over and pull the gown down over her legs. I look at the drip. Just water. She looks drowsy though. Must be the mask. I take it off her face, which, like her hair, is done up fancy. She's conscious, but not very. I slide the drip out from the back of her hand.

I slap her gently on the cheek. "You alright?"

She murmurs something I can't make out.

So I turn my attention to Pavel. Shaking off the tumble, he rises and draws a pistol. I'm on him fast. I smack it from his hand and throw him against the operating table. I crack my knuckles into fists.

He straightens his hair out. Removes his jacket and holster. Rests them on the edge of the table.

"Oh," I say, laughing, "fancy your chances, do you?"

Pavel steps out into some clear space in the room. He does some weird martial arts posturing. His legs wide and bent at the knees.

The guy's obviously got a death w—Christ, that hurt.

He catches me with a punch to the jaw. Didn't even see it. I swing a left. He dances around it and suckers me in the right kidney.

I take another fist to the ribs. Three in a row in fact. Rapid-fire blasts I can't stop. I'm down to one knee. Pavel waits. I get up. I swing again. He seizes my arm, twists it and elbows me in the spine. I throw a right. He's under it. Out of range. A step ahead.

As I turn, he side-kicks me. I stagger backwards against the operating table.

I gather myself. Ribs broken all over again. I hold a hand to my side, fighting for breath.

Pavel paces, staying loose. Dripping in smug. "What's wrong Charlie? Surprised I know how to fight?"

"I sank your bloody ship," I say, laughing, bleeding.

His nostrils flare. He lunges at me. Just what I wanted. I

get hold of him so he can't pick me off. But he's got other skills. And before I know what's happening, I'm on my back staring at those bright theatre lights.

The bastard must have judo-thrown me or something.

"Where'd you learn to fight like that?" I ask.

"Serbian special forces," Pavel says. "There's no shame in staying down."

"Just taking a breather," I say, rolling onto my front.

I get to my feet again, he hits me with a left and a right. Fast, efficient punches I can't telegraph. I swing and miss a couple more times. He drives a fist into my sternum. He kicks out my right knee and takes me down to the floor. He has the point of his hand on my throat. A knee on my right bicep. My left arm twisted to shit in a fancy torture hold.

He applies more pressure to my throat. Talks to me, quiet and close. "You're a persistent bastard, Charlie, but you're an ape. A dumb, blundering animal. You lack the training or finesse." Pavel's got me. He's got me good. "See, I don't even need a weapon," he says.

He's right. I'm choking to death.

"Any last words?" he asks, as he slowly kills me.

Chapter 63

Actually, I do have a few words for Pavel. But with his hand on my windpipe, they come out as cough and splutter.

Pavel seems amused. "Sorry Charlie, what was—" He wheezes mid-sentence.

Probably 'cause I'm crushing his ribcage between my thighs. He gives up on choking me and struggles to get free—both hands attempting to prise himself out.

I clear my throat. "I said, Pavel, you talk too much."

I nut the bastard hard in the mouth. His lips stain with blood. I push him off. As I get to my feet, he spins on the floor and sweeps my legs from under me. I hit the deck and roll away.

Pavel darts past me and grabs a scalpel off the tray. He backs off with it, twisting it in his hand.

I look at the tray. There's another scalpel. I dunno how good Pavel is in a knife fight, but I'm betting he's better than me.

He rushes me fast. I grab the tool tray and tip it upside down. I whack Pavel in the throat with the hard edge of the tray. He staggers, coughing blood. I pull him in close. "How's that for finesse?" I ask him, reversing the scalpel into his side.

He cries out. I wind him in the stomach. Crack him in the nose. Pick him up and power-slam him on the edge of the operating table.

He falls off, groans and tries to crawl, pulling the scalpel out from his side. Blood spots the floor in his wake. He's fresh out of juice.

I roll him onto his back with a foot. I pull him up to a sitting position by his shirt collar. A clenched fist ready to spark him out.

"Out of the way, Charlie."

I turn to see Amira. On her feet in front of the bed. Swaying a little. Pavel's weapon in both hands.

I hold out a hand. "Give me the gun, Amira."

"Get out of the way," she says, training the gun on Pavel, hands shaking.

"You don't wanna do this," I say, letting go of Pavel. I stand and tread slow towards her.

Amira's eyes are fierce, her chest heaving. She speaks through gritted teeth. "I want to know how it feels."

"How what feels?"

"To see one of them die."

I step out of the way in case that trigger finger of hers gets a little too itchy. "Don't let them drag you down, Amira."

Amira shuffles forward. "Why not?"

"Because there's enough of us down here as it is. And this piece of shit knows who's behind all this. He can help us stop it, whether he likes it or not." I close in on Amira. "Come on, give me the gun."

For a brief moment, I think she's gonna pull the trigger. But she lowers the weapon. Lets out a tearful sigh. I take the gun off her.

"I thought you were dead," Amira says.

"Well, the jury's still out on that one," I say, flexing my back and cracking a few bones.

"How did you find me?"

I run a fingertip over my cheek and study the soot on the end. "I asked around—as politely as I could."

She stares at me, confused. "Why would you—?"

I shrug as I detach the clip from the gun. I rest both of them on the operating table. "Seemed like a good idea at the time."

Amira smiles. It drops at the sight of something over my shoulder. I turn and see Pavel, rising to his feet. A gun detached from a velcro strap around his ankle.

I push his arm away as he shoots.

He misses. I reach out instinctively. Pick up a pair of surgical scissors off the tool stand. I drive the blades deep into his left temple.

Pavel's body goes loose. He drops the ankle pistol. Blood streams down his neck. He looks at me and opens his mouth to speak.

He flops to his right. Hits the floor with a smack.

Amira steps forward. "Is he—?"

"As a dodo." I dig inside his jacket pockets and find Pavel's phone. It's unlocked.

Don't know many mafioso who do bother locking 'em.

I swipe through to his call list. Remembering the time of the first phone call he took during my interrogation. There's a name next to the relevant time: Mr G. I dial the number. It rings a few times.

I hear a ringtone out in the corridor, through the doors. It's only faint, but it rings out in sync with the dial tone. I pop the clip in Pavel's main weapon. "Stay here a moment," I say, handing the ankle gun to Amira. "If anyone tries to operate on you, shoot 'em."

Amira grips the pistol tight in both hands and sits on the edge of the bed.

"Shouldn't be long," I say. "Then we'll clear this place out."

I push through the operating room doors. Mr G answers in Pavel's language. His voice baritone, mature.

"You speak English?" I ask.

"Who is this?"

I turn right and follow the sound of his voice to the end of the corridor.

"Hello?" Mr G says. "I said, who is this?"

As I peep around the corner, I see him stood with two bodyguards in black suits. He's a stocky guy in a roll neck jumper and a matching black raincoat. Big brown glasses and greying hair oiled back over his head. He hangs up and says something foreign to the bodyguards.

I take 'em by surprise and round the corner, my gun on 'em before anyone can draw. "Everyone relax," I say.

"Where's Pavel?" Mr G asks.

"Having a lie down."

The bodyguards step in front of their boss.

"You just made the biggest mistake of your life," Mr G says. "I'd suggest you disappear while you can."

"And I'd suggest you let the man with the gun make the demands."

I can see the bodyguards' hands twitching. Wanting to go for their weapons.

"What do you want?" Mr G asks.

"We'll get to that. Tell your boys to step aside."

"Or you'll do what?" says Mr G.

"Or I'll—"

The stairwell door to my left opens. In walks a bald copper in full uniform. "My wife's on her way—" he says, freezing. I see the name on his badge: *Chief Superintendent Bridlington.*

As he enters the conversation, one of the bodyguards draws.

Chapter 64

As one bodyguard goes for his weapon, the other throws himself into me. We wrestle for control of the gun. I direct the shot at the other bodyguard. It hits him in the arm. He draws his weapon with the other hand and pulls the trigger. I use the guy I'm fighting as a human shield. I run him towards the other guard. He takes another three rounds in the back. I push the guy off me. Beat the remaining bodyguard to the next shot. He collapses too. A bullet in the forehead.

That leaves Mr G and Bridlington.

Correction. Bridlington is already gone, through the stairwell door he came in through.

Mr G makes a dash towards the same exit. I sidestep and cut off his escape. He skids to a stop in his tan leather shoes. Doubles back, looking for another way out. I stride after him. He's got nowhere to go.

But he gets lucky. There's a sliding glass door out onto a large balcony. Wood decking, chairs and plants.

I'm thinking it's a tactical mistake. He'll end up running

into a dead end. But again, he gets the rub of the green. A metal staircase leads up onto the roof of the building.

Mr G heads up the stairs, his feet rattling off old iron steps. I go after him, but lose sight of the bastard.

I hit the top step and emerge onto the roof. No sign of Mr G, but I'd bet any money he's hiding out here somewhere.

I see a cluster of shafts and air conditioning units.

Any money he's behind one of 'em.

I tread light and fast. Creep around the back of an air conditioning unit, ready to jump out on him.

But Mr G is no fool. He double-bluffs me. Comes at me from behind. Signalled by a crack to the small of the back with something heavy. I stagger forward, down to one knee. Another whack to the wrist knocks the gun from my hand. It falls into the mouth of a ventilation shaft in the roof. Clatters all the way down.

Mr G swings again: a length of lead pipe. I reach up and catch the end. I tear it from his grip. He panics and runs. Across the rooftop, frantic in his search for an escape route. The first thing I do is block his exit back the way we came up.

It forces him towards the far end of the roof. I walk after him with the pipe, letting the end drag across the floor. The boss stands with his coat tails flapping in the wind. He peers over the edge of the building. Looks back at me. *"Who are you?"*

I keep walking. Don't answer.

"You kill me and you're a dead man," he says.

I get closer. He sits down on the edge of the roof, pushes himself off and vanishes from sight.

Don't tell me he's . . . No, the rooftop doesn't end there. It angles downwards. Smooth slate tiles at sixty degrees. After that, a sheer drop of ninety feet. But there's only a six foot gap from this roof to the next one. If he can make that jump, he can scramble up it.

I'm guessing that's why he's on his arse, sliding down towards the outer edge of the building.

I drop the pipe and sit on the ledge.

You must be bloody nuts, Charlie.

I swing my legs over and follow him down the slope. The slates are slippy. I slide faster than him, trying to catch up. He sees me coming and responds. A slate comes loose under my feet. I almost lose my balance.

But I stay on the tails of his raincoat.

He makes it down to the edge. Sizes up the jump. Sees me almost on top of him. He goes for it.

The bastard jumps surprisingly well. He catches hold of a drainpipe and bumps off the wall.

My own momentum almost takes me over the edge. I dig my heels in and steady myself. I avoid eye contact with the ground.

I push up into a crouch.

Sod it.

I make the jump.

Chapter 65

I land a foot to the left of Mr G, catching hold of the gutter.

He's already on the upward climb of slates, but he's close enough to kick me in the face. The gutter gives way under my weight. I slap a hand on the tiles. Another, hauling myself up onto my forearms.

Mr G kicks again. I catch his shoe. He pulls his leg away. The shoe slides off his foot in my hand. He scrambles up the rise. I let the shoe spiral to the ground. I fight with all the strength and grip I've got and make it onto all fours.

Roof tiles break off as Mr G climbs. A couple bounce into my face.

He slips and slides backwards. He hooks his arms around a pipe rising out of the roof.

I'm struggling for grip, too, out of breath. Mr G the same. He attempts to climb further. I dive forward and seize an ankle. I pull him towards me. He holds on for dear life to that pipe, stocky little legs kicking out against me.

I pull and pull until the pipe snaps. The pair of us tumble towards the edge. I grab the drainpipe as I fall. Mr G slides past me, but I catch him with my spare hand by the collar.

We come to a sudden stop. Me hanging off the pipe, my spare arm almost torn from the socket. Mr G hanging over the edge, only the stitching in his raincoat saving him from certain doom. The drainpipe is metal, thank Christ. I plant my right heel on the edge of the roof and get some leverage.

Mr G looks down at the drop. He swings, he panics. "Pull me up," he says.

"Hum, this is a well-made coat," I say. "How much does a coat like this cost?"

"What? Just fucking pull me up!"

"Why? So you can murder young women? Cut out the eyes of little kids? Uh-uh."

"Think about it," he says, "I can be a powerful friend to you."

The first stitch in his collar comes loose. Mr G doesn't look happy about it.

"I dunno." I say. "I've had friends like you before."

"I can make you rich," he says, eyeballing the ground. "Very rich."

The stitching rips some more. I struggle to keep hold of him.

Let him drop?

Pull him up?

If I don't decide in the next twenty seconds, gravity's gonna decide for me.

I look into those big, dark soulless glasses. "How rich?" I ask him.

Chapter 66

We stand outside departures. It's a warm day. The sun is shining.

Amira fiddles with the young girl's hair. The kid's name is Rima. She wears a pink coat and matching trainers. She smiles at Amira. A mouthful of tiny teeth. The colour's back in her cheeks again. Brown eyes twinkling in the light.

"There, now you look like a princess," Amira says, out of the escort dress and into jeans, a white sweater and a navy jacket.

A car approaches from the left. A sleek, black Audi saloon. It pulls up in front of us. The driver winds down his window. He's a young, blonde guy dressed in a smart grey suit and black tie.

"Charles Cobb?" he asks.

"That's me."

The driver takes a package from the passenger seat and hands it through the window. I pass the package onto Amira.

The driver hands me a clipboard and pen. Some kind of form. "Sign to confirm receipt," he says.

I scrawl something illegible at the bottom of the form. I hand it back. He nods and drives away.

I pick up Amira's travel case and the lady bird case I picked out for Rima. I pull theirs and mine in through the terminal doors. I help them find the right line for their flight to Munich, Amira's original destination.

She has a cousin there. He owns a small restaurant.

"He says I can help out in the kitchen," she says.

"Waiting on tables?" I say, rolling my eyes.

"It's a start," she says. "That's all we need."

"Well you'd better get going," I say.

Amira prompts Rima in Arabic. Rima dashes forward and hugs my right leg. I pat her on the head and try to shake her off me.

The kid finally lets go.

Amira comes in next for a brief hug. "I don't know how to thank you," she says in my ear.

"Ah, never mind all that bollocks," I say, breaking the hug. I look at Rima. "Shit, shouldn't swear in front of the kid."

Amira laughs. "It's fine. She doesn't understand."

"Everything there?" I ask, pointing to the envelope the driver handed over. "Papers? Passports?"

Amira pulls out two passports. She holds them up for me to see. "All here," she says. "But I don't understand . . . The passports, the visas, getting Rima out of hospital. How did you manage all this, Charlie?"

I smile. "A powerful friend," I say.

Chapter 67

Detective Clarke stopped the car across the road from the NAC building. His suit trousers still damp. The smell of carcinogens and river water up his nose.

"How are we gonna write this one up, guv?" Morales asked, toying with her straggled hair.

"Simple. We followed an anonymous tip," Clarke said. "We saved some girls from a sinking ship."

"And what about the guns?"

"Don't worry, they're in the river."

Clarke turned off the engine and unclipped his seatbelt. He caught Morales staring into the near distance.

"What the f—?" she said.

Clarke followed her line of sight towards a handful of detectives. They seemed to be discussing something outside the entrance to the building. Clarke and Morales climbed out of the car and wandered across the road.

As they approached, they caught sight of a man lying on his side on the pavement. The man wore a black raincoat and dark-brown glasses. His hands and feet bound, and mouth gagged with silver electrical tape. He mumbled and squirmed, a business card and a folded note peeping out of the breast pocket of his coat.

Detective Clarke pushed his way to the front. He kneeled down and plucked the card and note from the man's pocket.

He looked at the business card: one of his own. He turned it over and saw something scrawled in blue biro: *The scumbag you're looking for.*

He opened the note. It was addressed to him, with a shopping list of demands, scribbled in the same handwriting as the card.

Clarke scanned the list.

The author didn't leave a name, but he hardly needed to. He wanted documents and passports. And he'd left instructions on when and where to deliver them. A phone number too. And something about a hospitalised girl.

On delivery, the note said, Clarke would get a name. The name of his mole.

Chapter 68

My phone rings.

My other phone. Another cheap-as-chips burner with a number I gave to Clarke.

He's on the other end. A happy little pig rolling around in his own shit.

"You unwrap my present?" I ask.

"Edgar Grezda," he says. "Albanian Mafia."

"He talking yet?" I ask.

"He will," Clarke says.

"And the people in the clinic?"

"The patients are in care. The staff are being questioned."

"Well, make it stick," I say. "Don't let 'em off the hook."

"Don't worry, Charlie. Everyone wants a win on this one. Top Brass. High Court. Parliament. The whole lot."

"And this Grezda," I say. "He's a big fish?"

"He's a prize, but I think we can get a plea bargain. Reel in someone bigger."

"The thought of him getting off—bloody grates on me," I say.

"Grates on all of us," Clarke says. "But you know the game, Charlie. The higher we go . . ."

"Yeah, I get it," I say. "So what about me? Am I home free, or what?"

"Not exactly," Clarke says. "You've annoyed some powerful people. They've got your face and name, Charlie."

"And you lot?"

"Gotta come after you, I'm afraid."

"Huh. Wouldn't expect anything less."

"I've stalled things the best I can," Clarke says. "But you've only got a few hours until the manhunt kicks in. After that, they'll shut down the stations and airports."

"I'll be long gone by then," I say.

"You get your passports? Your documents?"

"All sorted," I say. "There's one thing I wanna know, though. At the hospital. Did you leave those paperclips on purpose?"

"I don't know what you're talking about," Clarke says.

"Yeah, that's what I thought."

"Anyway . . ." Clarke says, waiting.

"Oh the name, nearly forgot" I say. "It's Bridlington."

"Bridlington?" Clarke says. "You sure?"

"I saw him at the clinic, with Grezda. And my friend, Amira—she was in the room with 'em."

"His wife has a heart condition," Clarke says.

"From what Amira said, he's been trading favours to pay for private healthcare. And willing to skip the waiting lists for a transplant." Clarke goes quiet as he takes in the implications. "I suppose on one level, you can't blame the man," I say. "You know him?"

"Oh, I know him," Clarke says. "Good luck, Charlie."

I hang up and leave Detective Clarke to another fresh mess. Never thought I'd end up working with a copper. Never thought I'd grow to like him. I suppose they're not all bad.

As a cleaner pushes a cart by me, I slip the burner inside an open rubbish bag. I hear the roar of distant jet engines. See a 747 climbing steep into the blue London skies. I pull my small, black travel case through a set of automatic doors, into Terminal 3. Different to the one I dropped Amira and Rima off at.

It's still early, but Heathrow is nice and busy. Easy to disappear. I stop below a bank of departure screens. I look through the flight times and destinations.

Britain's out.

Eastern Europe, too.

And the Albanian lot are bound to come looking for me in Spain.

But there's a whole world I've never explored. Asia, Africa, Australia, America.

All the A's.

I make a snap decision. I ask if there are any seats going spare at an airline booking desk. Turns out I'm in luck. A friendly blonde woman tells me there's a flight leaving in an hour. And there's one spot left on the plane— a last-minute deal.

"I'll take it," I say, lifting my case onto the scales.

She books me onto the flight and hands me my ticket.

I thank her and move on. I take a look around me,

checking my surroundings. Not a copper or mobster in sight.

With nothing but a passport in hand, I melt into the crowd. And I'm gone.

Guide to Charlie Cobb & UK Slang

Bloke - Man
Bollocks - Expression of frustration / testicles
Boozer - Pub
Burner - Disposable phone
Butty - Sandwich
Brew - Cup of tea
Chippy - Fish & Chip shop
Cig - Cigarette
Dickhead - Foolish or annoying person
Geez / Geezer - Man, or male friend
Goon - hench-person
Jizz - Semen
Knackered - Exhausted or Broken
Lad - boy, male teen or young man
Love - way of addressing a stranger
Mate - friend (may not be a friend)
Muff - Vagina / Prostitutes
Narky - irritable, snarky, snide
Nick - Steal

Old Bill - Police
Pal - friend (may not be a friend)
Pig(s) - Police officer(s)
Piss - Urine / Urinate
Prossies - Prostitutes
Puff - cannabis, smoked
Roller - Rolls Royce
Slaphead - follically-challenged individual
Strangeways - High security prison in Manchester, UK
Tea - Dinner / Evening meal (also means cup of . . .)

Also by Rob Aspinall

Breaker (Charlie Cobb #1)
Homecoming
Truly Deadly
Infinite Kill (Truly Deadly #2)
World Will Fall (Truly Deadly #3)
Made of Fire (Truly Deadly #4)

Connect with Rob

Did you enjoy the book?

I'd love to hear what you think. Please leave an online review wherever's convenient. Your honest feedback will make a huge difference. Thanks for sharing.

Follow Rob:

Instagram: rob_aspinall
Facebook: facebook.com/robaspinallauthor
Twitter: @robaspinall

More about the author:

www.robaspinall.com

Printed in Great Britain
by Amazon